# Simple Steps to Photographic Memory

## Even the average Joe can do it now.

STEFAN CAIN

Although the author and publisher have made every effort to ensure that the information in this book was correct at press time, the author and publisher do not assume and hereby disclaim any liability to any party for any loss, damage, or disruption caused by errors or omissions, whether such errors or omissions result from negligence, accident, or any other cause.

# DEDICATION

Our best shoots are placed in our memory. They are simply there, somewhere .. and they represent our private archive... Nobody can touch .. nobody can see.

**Massimo Conti**

This page intentionally left blank.

# Contents

This page intentionally left blank.

# 1

---

## ENCODING FOR MEMORY STORAGE

What is MEMORY? Is it possible to develop a PHOTOGRAPHIC MEMORY? (Or at least come across like you do?) How does memory work? Why does it work so inconsistently? Can you remember what you forgot?

You are capable of recalling and retaining more information than you imagine. Your long-term memory is very powerful, though it is all too often taken for granted. After all, hypnotists have been known to retrieve memories from your mind that you have long since forgot. Obviously, that information has been there all along - you simply lacked the proper means of retrieving those memories.

Memory has three basic functions: Encoding, Storage, and Retrieval. When you see an infant in the crib, the child is watching, listening, touching and moving, making noises. The baby's mind is a blank slate, but he or she is over-alert. Clinical studies have been performed which showed that infants have learned to recognize their own mothers, as opposed to other women. This was proven using brain scans. Babies see, hear, and notice everything!

Babies are **encoding**. During their waking hours, they are constantly absorbing information gleaned via their senses. They will touch the sides of their cribs, squeeze their teddy bears, look at the mobile you have clamped to the crib, listen to the tune, hear the chirping of birds outside and look at them. They are kicking their legs, sucking their thumbs, smelling the supper cooking on the stove, watching and looking everywhere. No wonder babies sleep so much! They are in a condition of information overload and exhaustion!

## MEMORY ENCODING

The term **encoding** is now often used to mean putting information into that electronic animal known as the computer. It is input in the form of a cryptic code in which only a computer maven could decipher. Computer encoding is composed of natural numbers, capital letters, and punctuations put into sets called a code space consisting of bits, octets, code sets, and patterns like:

### 2601:1C2:1300:D091:1FA:2FFD:DACE:D98]
### yadda...yadda...yadda...

The human brain also encodes data every day in its own peculiar way. It perceives and automatically accepts some data and blows off the fluff into the winds of nothingness. Your computer stores all of the data – the useful data, the ancillary data, the false data, and the useless data. Then it runs out of memory! David Chalmers, a contemporary philosopher, has warned people that computers will become more intelligent than humans, and that day is close at hand. Rest assured – that Computer Armageddon, if it does come, is light years away! Your brain has the ability to record <u>useful</u> data. Sadly though, some useful data "leaks out" and that is why you came here.

**Consolidation** – Information that enters the brain is **categorized**. Individuals make judgments as to the nature of the input, and ready it for the short-term or long-term memory. For example, if you hear a bird chirp, you dismiss it immediately. It is amusing to note that if you were to type "is" instead of "its" in a document, your computer will regurgitate the error. In fact, it will still be stored long after it is corrected! That is how the FBI may retrieve "deleted" information!

## Learning Styles: How Do You Learn?

The means by which information is encoded is through sensory perception. Everyone has their own preferred ways of learning, favoring one or more of the senses to record information. These are called "Learning Styles."

There is an old adage first uttered by William Mellin in 1957: **"Garbage in…garbage out."** Although its original application was applied to computer science, it is also true of humans. It is the result of the absorption (or encoding) of false data, or falsely recording accurate data. For example, a father takes his three-year old boy to the ice cream vendor. His son orders a hot fudge sundae. He receives a hot fudge sundae with nuts on it, as is customary. His Dad orders a hot fudge ice cream sundae with "no nuts." His father gets a hot fudge sundae with chocolate sprinkles on it. (Courteously substituted for the nuts) His little boy looks at the chocolate sprinkles. He remembers that they looked good. The next time, he and his father go to a *different* ice cream store. The little one orders a hot fudge sundae with "no nuts," and he receives a hot fudge sundae with no nuts, but without chocolate sprinkles on it. Then the child complains bitterly and says to his Dad: "Where are the <u>no nuts</u>?" (A long father-son discussion follows, leaving the father totally confused!)

That very simplistic mishap is the result of improper encoding. Here the little boy learned <u>visually</u> and <u>aurally</u> by associating the visual image of chocolate sprinkles with the sound of the words "no nuts." Of course, once the father was able to point out the chocolate sprinkles on his ice cream sundae and say the proper words, the child understood.

One of the most popular learning styles is called the **VAK/VARK Model** and it was developed by William Barbe et al, in 1981, and expanded by Neil Fleming in 1987.

## VAK/VARK MODEL OF LEARNING STYLES

**Visual** – This learning style employs visual aids such as images, maps, charts, graphs, and related graphic devices. A person who tends to form mental images, even from abstract concepts, prefers this style.

**Aural** – This style uses hearing and speech to help with information encoding. When a person uses sounds to encode information, he or she may say words aloud or mentally in order to encode the input.

**Read/Write** – Textual-based input is the basis for encoding. In this case, the person reads and writes the words on a notepad or a computer device.

**Kinesthetic** – This occurs when a person learns through the use of practical examples, or by trial-and-error. It is through tactile means that one learns.

### Determine Your Learning Style: Introductory Exercise

Here is how to determine your learning styles. Read the passage below:

Upon the surrender of the Carthaginian Empire, Rome demanded money and that the people leave their beloved city of Carthage, surrender to the legions, and be sold as slaves. Horrified at the prospect, the people of Carthage refused. Upon hearing of this, Cato the Elder leaped from his stone bench in the Senate and bellowed: *"Carthage must be destroyed!"*

Coveting fame and fortune, young Scipio, the adopted grandson son of the revered Punic War hero, Scipio Africanus, decided to deliver Rome's final retaliation. His regiment forged ahead through the searing desert toward Carthage. They brought siege engines, torches, long spears, and finely honed broadswords. Seeing the city gates in front of them, five and forty soldiers thrust the battering ram through the tall wooden doors. The

Roman legions roared as they rushed full force into the city. They were met by hordes of bearded Carthaginian with swords and spears held high. Furiously they battled each other mercilessly.

Huge stones rained down from above. Every building was a fortress. Flanks of Carthaginians poured boiling oil upon the Romans from the rooftops. It cascaded and splattered upon the soldiers below who howled in pain. Seeing that the battle had moved to the roofs, Scipio ordered in the siege engines. These formidable wooden towers were four stories high with steps leading from one floor to the next. An opening was on the top level to give the soldiers access to the tops of the buildings. There they met the enemies face-to-face. Swords clanked upon shields; shields clashed upon shields. Scipio thrust his sword into the stomach of one and pulled out his bloodied sword. It made a sickening sucking noise as it exited. Huge tongues of flame licked up from below. Consumed with rage, his solders fought valiantly until the rooftops were littered with broken bodies. The battle was over.

The roaring flames subsided, leaving wood and cloth in cinders. Scipio surveyed the once magnificent city, stepping over melted metal and heaps of the dead from both sides.

Surrounded with nothing but death and smoldering ruins, Scipio wept bitterly because there were no spoils to bring back to Rome. *

Do not reread the story until you ask yourself the question

below. <u>No answer is wrong; this is not a test</u>. It is simply a measure of preference.

What two aspects of the story fascinated you the most?
1. The visualizations of the battle, the heaps of dead corpses, crumbled stones and smoldering ruins

2. The sounds of the howling soldiers as they were covered with boiling oil, and the clashing of sword upon sword

3. The construction of the siege engine, how it worked, and the directional progress of the Roman legions

4. The words used to describe the event and the bird's eye view of Scipio's rooftop skirmish

If you liked #4 the best, you employ the **Read/Write** style the most. You like to see the whole picture, and break it up into relevant portions. You tend to take notes either mentally, by writing them down, or recording them on mobile devices.

If you liked #3, you are captivated by the kinetics of the situation. You would like to examine the siege engine close-up and map out movements of soldiers as they dashed across planks from rooftop to rooftop. This is characteristic of the **Kinesthetic** style.

If you liked #2, you are drawn to the auditory features of the piece. If you "heard" the imaginary crackling of the flames, the howling of the soldiers drenched in scalding oil, then you relate best to hearing something and repeating it in order to ascertain full comprehension. You prefer the **Aural** style of learning.

If you liked #1, you prefer to visualize things. You could "see" the soldiers in your mind, the tongues of flames licking the building's walls, and the piles of corpses lying on the cobblestones. You prefer the **Visual** style.

No doubt, you have a second favorite style. Take note of that. Those two styles should be utilized to increase your memory power.

*Passage is a fictionalized account of the fall of Carthage in 146 BC, adapted from the writings of Polybius (200 BC-118 BC) and Plutarch (46 AD-120 AD).

# 2

—

# EXERCISES IN ENCODING

Most people learn by favoring one of the sensory learning styles over the others. However, you can enhance your memory skills if you try to engage more than one learning strategy. It would be wise if you could try your favorite style first, and then engage a different style to accompany it. For example, if you tend to recall the printed word, you might try to simultaneously engage some mental imaging to accompany your reading.

## Visual Learning Style: Exercises to Enhance Memory

1. Watch and record a TV show. Make an extra effort to notice the backgrounds. Try to remember them. Play the show back and check to see how well you did. Undercover agents, police, and soldiers spend a great deal of training time developing their observational skills. One of the most essential of these, of course, is how to distinguish friend from foe in a fraction of a second.

2. Get a small flashlight, turn it on, and take off your watch.

Hold the watch in your hand and shine the flashlight on it. Rotate the watch and analyze it visually. Put the flashlight and watch on your desk.

Close your eyes, and form a mental image of it. In your mind, rotate it and try to identify how and where it glittered. Open your eyes and repeat the exercise to compare the real image with your mental one.

3. Close your eyes. What other items were on your desk? Open your eyes and check. What did you miss? (This was a sneaky question!)

4. Close your eyes. Imagine a woodland scene. Open your eyes. Without making it up, what kind of day was it? What was on the ground when you imagined it?

5. Close your eyes, and put more details into your mental picture. Put yourself in it. With your mind's eye, listen. Smell. Feel the ground. You have engaged your visual senses, your auditory senses, your olfactory senses, and your tactile sensations. The image is now much more complete.

6. Close your eyes. Put yourself back in the woodlands. Add someone, and carry on a brief conversation with him or her. Open your eyes and write down the conversation. You have now employed the read/write style of encoding.

7. In less than an hour, recall your woodland experience. Go over it in your mind.

In performing #7, you have now moved your woodland adventure from your short-term to your long-term memory.

That is because information recall needs rapid reinforcement in order to be retrieved at a future time. Have you ever noticed how college students quickly review their books and notes right before taking their exams? It works. Tonight and tomorrow, and perhaps even a week later, you will remember your woodland experience. Guaranteed!

## Aural Learning Style: Exercises to Enhance Memory

1. Keep your eyes closed during this entire exercise. Listen. Make it a point to hear *everything*. Keep your eyes closed and state out loud what you heard. Now listen again to check for accuracy.

2. Find an instructional YouTube video about something you might enjoy. Something light. Close your eyes and listen to it for a full five minutes. Open your eyes and pause it. Paraphrase what you heard.

3. Return to the beginning of the video and listen to it for about 2-3 minutes. Memorize what the speaker said. Say it aloud. Return to the beginning of the video, close your eyes, and check to see if you got it right.

4. Locate a musical soundtrack on the Internet. Choose something you do not recognize. Play it for about five minutes. Stop it and try to recall it. Try to sound it out. Return to the beginning and try it again.

5. Locate a new soundtrack. Bookmark the page on your browser. Play the soundtrack for about five to ten minutes.

Make it a point to hear the background music as well as the melody. Put it on pause and
try to sing it or hum the melody. Now try to sound out the rhythm you heard in the background. (That is the tricky part!) Play it back to check.

6. Play it again, and imagine you are one of the musicians. Imagine what the instruments look like and imagine what the musicians look like as well. In your mind, touch your instrument, and play it along with the other musicians. Stop the recording and write down what the instruments were. If you miss one or two, return to the recording and correct yourself.

7. In less than an hour, recall your musical escapade. You will now remember it for quite some time because you have converted a short-term memory to a long-term memory. You may even remember it for a week or more!

What you have done is to expand your aural learning style to a visual, tactile (kinesthetic), and the read/write style. That reinforces memory.

## Read/Write Learning Style: Exercises to Enhance Memory

1. Select a multi-paragraph piece to read. Select a relatively short passage of 6-8 paragraphs each and read it.

2. Underline the keyword(s) in each paragraph and attach at least one verb to each word. Write down just the keywords. Glance over your list.

3. In a sentence or two using your own words, write down the general gist of the passage. Try to use some of the keywords you noted. Check your work against the original paragraphs, and see if there is something missing.

4. Without referring to the original piece, write out a longer essay. Check your work and redo if needed.

5. Select a page to a page and a half from a novel and read it. It does not have to be from the initial pages.

6. Write down (or take mental notes) of the character names, and associate an action verb or a description of each character's intent at the time. Write them down (or take mental notes).

7. Ask yourself: *"What is the gist of the story so far?"* Compare your answer to the original text. If you were not correct, redo.

8. Ask yourself: *"What is the setting for what I read?"* Check to see if you were accurate. Most likely you are! That section of the story is now committed to your short-term memory. If you review it in about 1-2 hours, it will be remembered for a longer time.

**Kinesthetic Learning Style: Exercises to Enhance Memory**

People who use the kinetic as a learning style also tend to employ the visual style of learning as well which will serve a supportive purpose. For example, when plumbers come to replace or repair your kitchen drainpipe, they will first look under your sink. The most experienced among them will already know the size of the pipes, the joints, and the general configuration, just by cursory visual observation.

1. Locate a map that clearly shows the countries bordering the Black Sea, and examine it. On a table, assemble 7 objects – three of which will be a tad larger like a saltshaker, a peppershaker, and a juice glass. On the four smaller objects use items such as shot glasses, beans, or similar.

2. Referring to your map, place the objects around an empty oval that signifies an imaginary Black Sea. Use the larger items for Russia, Turkey, and the Ukraine and situate them in place along the Black Sea. Add on the smaller objects to represent Georgia, Romania, Moldova, and Bulgaria. Study your configuration and compare it to the map.

3. Hide the map, and mix up the objects. See if you can do it again without referring to the map. Check the map to assess your results. Correct and redo if necessary.

4. For your second exercise, read a page about the late Renaissance (or another historical period). Draw 3 columns. In the left column you will write the dates. In the middle column, write important keywords – mostly nouns (they can be just keyword nouns, persons, or places). In the third column, write down a verb or adjective about each keyword. You like structures, and you have now designed the historical period structurally. Review your list for accuracy.

5. Without referring to the passage or your list, draw your three columns. Put the dates you recall on the left, the keyword nouns go in the second column, and the descriptive words goes in the third column. Check the original text and compare. Redo if

needed, and study it.

6. Now write out or recite the information in essay form. You should be able to do this quite easily.

It is most helpful for people to practice exercises in learning styles in other categories as well. For example, a visually oriented person might try an exercise that favors the kinesthetic style of learning. Becoming flexible in using different kinds of learning style will boost your memory power.

The philosophers who advocated empiricism and phenomenology always focused upon sensation as the primary means by which people learn. They believed that perception was the first step in arriving at knowledge and truth. The learning styles addressed in the first two chapters depend exclusively upon your senses. This is how you learn; it is how you remember, and it the way in which you structure your reality.

## Curious Facts About the Olfactory Sense

The sense of smell is also a sensation. Unlike sensations derived from your other senses, the memory of a smell tends to make a deeper impression. This sense dates back to the human being living in prehistoric times. It is genetic. At that time, human beings depended upon the sense of smell for their survival. For example, the odor of a herd of wild animals, the smell of sweet fruit, the smell of cooking food were if prime importance. The most basic need anyone has is the instinctual need for survival. Yes, smells do fade after a short time, but the memory of them lasts much longer. If it is an alarming odor, like that of a large gasoline leak, burning, or even the odor of a dead body, that smell only has to be "learned" once and is immediately filed in your long-term memory.

Believe it or not, some very accomplished naturalists have learned how to smell animals. You, too, possess that ability! If you take a sniff at the groundhog's hole, you will sense the odor of a wild animal! Of course, you need to stoop down and smell at nearly ground level to catch the odors of small animals. If you just bend over a bit and sniff, you may even catch the odor of deer who have recently passed by. If you will notice, dogs hold their noses down toward the ground, and then sometimes lift their heads a bit to sense the smell of larger animals and people. Of course, dogs have many more olfactory nerves than people do.

## ASSOCIATIVE LEARNING AND MEMORY

Memory depends a great deal upon associations. Items seen every day is associated with other objects that are usually nearby and have a relationship - an association. A computer is associated with word processing, database management, communications, graphical analysis, and the like. Any one of those items will remind you of a computer. A tree is associated with its structure: trunk, branches, leaves, and green. Similarities are also recalled. For example, if you see something that is just a 6-inch hard stem with a leaf emerging from the ground, you will conclude that it is a young tree.

If you did the exercise for #1-3 for the **Kinesthetic** learning style, you will associate any one of those countries with the

Black Sea. If someone was to say "Poland" to you, you know that it does NOT border the Black Sea.

# 3

---

# INFORMATION STORAGE

## Your Control of Your Brain

People tend to take their brains and their minds for granted, like how you take your fingers for granted. Try this:

---

1. Put your right arm at your side.

2. Mentally concentrate on your hand.

3. Intensify your concentration.

4. Are your fingers tingling? Are they vibrating a bit?

---

Yes, they are. You and your brain have more control of your conscious awareness than you may have formerly believed. This is a belief adopted by those who have or appear to have a photographic memory.

Before any memorization, concentrate on your brain. This may sound silly, but you can conduct a simple test to prove you can direct your focus there and stimulate it! Try this:

---

1.  Concentrate on your cerebral cortex (front and top of your head)

2.  Do you *"feel"* it? You will perceive a "full" sensation.

---

This may sound gruesome, but scientists have studied the brains of the deceased, including Einstein's. The physical appearance of the brains was NOT different, even for those who had photographic memories. Only in the case of brain tumors or lesions will there be a biological difference; however, that is not related to intelligence.

You have a brain that is not different from a person who has a photographic memory. All of its areas function just like those of the super-intelligent. It helps to know the areas of the brain because there is a part of your brain that can be taught to stimulate your mind. On the popular front, it is called mind control. Use it and be aware of the areas of the brain that are activated when you are learning and memorizing.

The frontal area of your brain is called the **Prefrontal Lobe.** It makes decisions, receives and processes information, and is responsible for your higher mental functioning. It will also analyze and process memories. It **encodes** information such as was discussed in Chapter 1. The area of your brain that sits just behind the prefrontal lobe is called the **Parietal Lobe**. It interprets sensations that are the initial sources of your learning. Both the Prefrontal Lobe and the Parietal Lobe will send signals to your hippocampus.

If you hold up your index finger to your ear lobe and point inwards, the **Hippocampus** lies deep inside toward the center of your brain. It is a circular-like structure. This is the area responsible for determining whether a memory should be relegated to **short-term memory** or **long-term memory.** That is, you determine whether or not you want to retain a memory over the short-term or over a longer period of time.

As a simple example, you see that your coffee maker has completed its cycle, and the coffee is ready. Your mind forms an image of a cup of coffee, and sends signals to your muscles to go grab a mug. Your hippocampus has relegated this to short-term memory. However, you have learned where the coffee machine is, and that becomes part of your long-term memory. The information in your long-term memory is stored in various parts of your brain.

There are bean-sized structures at the very base of your hippocampus that apprehend emotions. That area is called the **Amygdala.** The feeling that you associate with an image or a thought is often accompanied by an emotional impression. For example: "nice-nasty", "pleasant-unpleasant", and "anger-fear. An unbalanced diet, fatigue, lack of exercise, and emotions such as chronic depression, anxiety and fear will interfere with memory.

# THE ROLE OF NEUROTRANSMITTERS AND HORMONES IN MEMORY PROCESSING

Neurotransmitters are chemicals that bounce from one nerve cell ("neuron") to another across what are called synapses. Hormones are molecules that are released from glands in your body and shot into your bloodstream for distribution to certain parts of your body. Sometimes, neurotransmitters work hand-in-hand with hormones. Neurotransmitters are properties of your nervous system. Hormones are properties of your endocrine system. Thus, a thought in your mind will transmit a signal to other nerves that will trigger a response. The responses can be <u>active</u> such as singing a song for which you need to remember the tune. This would involve both a neurotransmitter and a hormone. The responses can be more <u>passive</u>, such as looking at a map of Europe, and producing a mental image of the map. This would involve just a neurotransmitter and takes place in the brain.

The neurotransmitters utilized by your brain are:

- Glutamate
- Acetylcholine
- Norepineprine and Epinephrine
- Dopamine
- GABA
- Histamine
- Serotonin

**Glutamate** is the major neurotransmitter contributing to learning and memory acuity. As an excitatory neurotransmitter, it triggers the secretion of an amino acid – a protein called glutamic acid. This is used by your brain and has been popularly termed "brain fuel." Production of glutamic acid can be enhanced with the proper dietary ingredients. Dietary suggestions that intensify memory functions will be discussed in Chapter 8.

**Acetylcholine** is an excitatory neurotransmitter that not only fires up your muscles, but also keeps you awake and attentive. When you have a sufficient amount of it in your system, you will feel energetic; this is conducive to learning and memory. Easy exercises to promote the continual production of acetylcholine will be in Chapter 8.

**Norepineprine and Epinephrine** are excitatory neurotransmitters that not only provide you with energy, but also stimulate attentiveness. They are excitatory neurotransmitters that release the hormones, adrenaline and cortisol from the adrenal glands above your kidney. Attention is a major factor in the encoding of experiences. Norepinephrine and epinephrine can have deleterious effects in the case of overstimulation because they accept direct input from your emotional centers. Anxiety is one of the factors that can reverse the positive effects of norepinephrine and epinephrine. A synthesized form of epinephrine is often administered to people whose hearts have stopped beating due to a heart attack.

**Dopamine** is the major neurotransmitter that aids in attention. It also contributes to motivation because it is associated with reward. It can motivate you to employ your memory and will help you feel gratified when you realize that you were successful in recalling a fact or experience. Certain foods will stimulate the production of dopamine. It must be in proper ratio to serotonin (see below).

**GABA** is sometimes dubbed "nature's valium." It is an inhibitory neurotransmitter that has a calming effect on the human body, and reduces anxiety that interferes most significantly with memory functioning. Valerian root is the basis for some medical supplements that aid with its secretion.

**Histamine** as a neurotransmitter regulates your waking-sleeping cycle. No doubt you recognize the term to describe allergy-reduction medications. ("antihistamine") Too much histamine not only interferes with your waking and sleeping regulation, but causes the "sniffles."

**Serotonin** is the main regulatory neurotransmitter. It monitors the balance between excitatory and inhibitory responses.

## SHORT-TERM AND LONG-TERM MEMORY

Short-term memory, sometimes called "working memory," means what the words imply. The information absorbed is only held for a short time, possibly even just seconds or minutes. Most people who have poor memory are using their short-term memory without making the effort to commit it to long-term memory. The hippocampus in the brain is responsible for allocating a fact to either short-term or long-term memory. Who needs a "lazy" hippocampus?

There are several factors involved in creating the long-term memory of a fact or an event. If one or more of those factors is overlooked, the information will be stored in the "circular file" (the waste basket)!

Factors:

- Environment
- Motivation
- Emotional Status
- Biological Needs, e.g., you are hungry or ill
- Self-Esteem

For the most part, these are obvious. However, self-esteem may not be. For years perhaps you have been feeding yourself with irrational beliefs about your memory skills. The psychologist, Albert Ellis, used the rational-emotive approach to help his clients change their attitudes about themselves. He indicated that they tend to compose beliefs about themselves that are simply irrational. With reference to your ability to remember information, you might be telling yourself one or more of the following:

1. I have a rotten memory.
2. I never remember people's names.
3. I would "forget my head if it was not attached"!
4. Everyone else remembers things better than I do.
5. People think I am dumb.
6. I am easily confused.
7. I am subject to brain fade.
8. This is boring.
9. No one can understand this stuff!
10. I am a total failure!

If you adopt these attitudes, you have dealt a severe blow to your ego. What is more destructive is the fact that defeatist beliefs can become self-fulfilling prophecies. **A person, who has decided that he or she cannot remember names, WILL NOT remember them!**

Create some positive affirmations for yourself. Believe them, and it will be so!

In the next two sections, you can learn how to beat the odds, and transfer your short-term memories to long-term ones.

## EBBINGHAUS CURVE OF FORGETTING

This study showed that humans tend to forget nearly half of what they remember within a week. Much of that is due to the fact that facts are committed to short-term memory first. After that, it may or may not be relegated to long-term memory. When you want to remember some things you are planning to do over the course of a week or month, it would certainly be handy in terms to help you proceed in a more organized fashion. It can be an aid when you attend a party and are introduced to new people.

# Tips for Reducing Rapid Forgetfulness

- Strengthen your **initial attentiveness** during the initial encoding period.
- **Review** the material within an hour of receiving it.
- Review again and again. This is called **overlearning**.
- Make note of the fact that you will tend to remember the first and last item better than those items in between. Compensate for that by **altering the order** of the facts and review them accordingly.
- **Avoid multitasking.**
- Utilize **imagery.**
- **"Chunking"** of like items into meaningful categories. (See below)
- Play **Sudoku** or card games.
- Make it a goal to **finish what you start.**
- Learn **something new** every day. It does not have to be important. It could be something as simple as a new word.
- **Vary** your day. Avoid doing the same types of tasks over and over <u>ad nauseum</u>.
- If you have a sedentary job, get up and **walk** around from time to time.
- **Meditate** (See Chapter 6)
- Drink                                                                      **water**

If you want to improve your memory, it is essential that you alter your manner of thinking. You should use this approach to any memory task. Use this anagram: **FUROR**. F– **Focus**; **Understand**; **Recall**; **Organize**; **Review**.

**Focus** - Focus upon the material. Close out all distracting stimuli. If you are aurally inclined, by all means play some music. Other people prefer quiet. If you are kinesthetically inclined, do something that requires some limited movement. Have you ever seen children in the first year of school? Although they may be sitting at their desks, they will move their legs and even their arms in no particular pattern. Children are kinesthetically inclined.

**Understand** – <u>Evaluate</u> the material at hand. <u>Analyze</u> it for associations or similarities. <u>Grasp</u> the whole theme of the paragraph or page.

**Recall** – Briefly remind yourself of the theme, and the meaning of the words in the content.

**Organize** – Place the material into sets of similar facts or words. (Associations)

**Review** – Go over the material in your mind briefly. Check it against the original and make corrections if necessary.

### Exercises – "Chunking"

In his famous study, George Miller, the psychologist, discovered that the number of unrelated items that could be recalled at one given time was only between 5-9! However, if you organize those items into groups, the amount of information retained is much greater. In her article for the *Encyclopedia of Human Behavior*, Amanda Gilchrist said: "Chunking is one of the most powerful strategies to increase the information we hold in our mind."

There are two ways of "chunking"

- Break up the units using dashes or some other separators. For example, a telephone number: 018-555-7951. This works far better than: 0185557951.
- Categorize words into coherent groups.

## Exercise A:

1. Break up the following numbers into groups: 65916236773
2. Commit them to memory
3. Write them down or record them. Check for accuracy and repeat if necessary.
4. In ten minutes, review your numbered sequence.

Step #4 will help you commit the numbers to memory for a longer period of time.

## Exercise B:

1. Look at these words, and examine them:

| Soda | Boxing |
| --- | --- |
| Noun | 1988 |
| Apple | Tennis |
| 2013 | Verb |
| Soccer | 2002 |
| Turnip | Adjective |

Check out an example of how these words can be chunked:

| Soda | Turnip | Apple |
|---|---|---|
| Boxing | Soccer | Tennis |
| Noun | Adjective | Verb |
| 2013 | 1988 | 2002 |

The words have been categorized or "chunked" into coherent rows: Food, Sports, Words, and Dates.

2. Now select some words of your own from a how-to piece or a cookbook. Repeat the activity above.

**Exercise C:**

This exercise is longer, but it is important to challenge yourself.

1. Instead of separating words into discrete categories, you can use keywords. In the following selection, zero in on the main categories. Those will be your main keywords. Read the brief synopsis of each. Make mental note of the keywords that could be traits or descriptions of the categories as you read:

The Bedouins are nomadic people who live on the Arabian Peninsula. They traditionally have herded camels and sheep. Later on, some became farmers.

The Berbers consist of a number of tribes who speak the Berber language. Most of them dwell in the Maghrib, which is in Northern Africa.

The Copts are Egyptians who belong to their own religious sect. They are Christians.

The Druze is a religious sect living in Syria, Jordan, and Lebanon. They follow Neo-Platonic ideals and believe in reincarnation.

The Ismailis of Hunza live in a mountainous area of Pakistan near the border of China. They dress very colorfully and speak their own language.

The Kurds live in an area of Northern Iraq originally called Kurdistan. They are herders, or farm and raise goats and sheep.

The Pashtuns are people who live on either side of the Pakistani-Afghan border. They maintain their own tribal customs, but have also adopted Muslim practices.

The Sufis live all over the Arab countries. They follow Islam for the most part, but are also mystics trained in the practices of meditation and spiritual union with Allah.

---

1. Go over the reading briefly.
2. Set up two columns for yourself.
3. In the left column, write own the keyword for each category.
4. In the right column, write down a very brief description. Use

as few words as possible.

5. Review the material, and check for accuracy.

6. Commit it to memory.

7. Review again.

---

In 20-40 minutes, review the material yet again. You have now committed the material to a longer-term memory. The degree of practice you apply to tasks like this will help you intensify your long-term memory faster and better than you were before.

# 4

---

# INTERMEDIATE EXERCISES –
# MEMORY STORAGE

Mnemonic devices are memory "tricks" you can employ to memorize information such as lists, people, places, objects, words, and the like. People who have photographic memories employ these devices.

*Note:* People with photographic memories do not necessarily have higher IQs than others, by the way!

## ACRONYMS

One of most frequently used devices is this rhyming series that uses visual imagery:

1 – Gun
2 – Shoe
3 – Tree
4 – Door
5 – Hive
6 – Kicks

7 – Heaven
8 – Gate
9 – Line
10 – Pen

## Exercise A:

Take this list of objects:

- Flashlight
- Cap
- Chair
- Pillow
- Lamp
- Umbrella
- Bathrobe
- Blanket
- Locomotive
- Bowl

Take the easy-to-remember rhyming series:

Gun, Shoe, Tree, Door, Hive, Kicks, Heaven, Gate, Line, Pen.

Now for the list, think of 1) **Gun:** A gun shooting off many flashlights, 2) **Shoe:** A shoe stuffed full of many, many caps, 3) **Tree:** A tree with many, many chairs hanging from it, 4) **Door:** A door opening up with many, many pillows popping out of it, 5) **Hive:** A hive with many lamps circling around it, 6) **Kicks:** A lower leg kicking many umbrellas up in the air, 7: **Heaven:**

Clouds with many bathrobes on them, 8: **Gate:** A gate opening up with many blankets behind it, 9: **Line:** A clothesline with many locomotives hanging from it, and 10) **Pen:** An animal pen filled with many bowls.

**Exercise B:**

Here is a list for you to do:

- Mirror
- Mat
- Book
- Bear
- Brush
- Cushion
- Ear buds
- Bobble head
- Magnifier
- Bracelet

## LETTER ACRONYMS

Another form of the acronym technique is the usage of the same letter or letters with a slight variation.

In any journalistic article, there are a number of features to be kept in mind when writing the piece. Those aspects will make the article more interesting and still get the point effectively delivered to the readers. Those features are characterized by the

**5 C's:** **C**lear, **C**ohesive, **C**omprehensible, **C**oncise, **And C**orrect.

Journalists also use an acronym to develop the factual and commentary sections of their articles. They use the formula for repeated letters with a variation: the **5 W's + 1 H:** **W**ho, **W**hat, **W**hen, **W**here, **W**hy, and **H**ow.

That is what they use for the "lede" (lead) in their story.

## WORD TYPE ACRONYMS

Journalists also intend to compose their stories based on inclusion of these elements:

**P**urpose - Goal?
**A**udience – Kinds of readers. Historians? Children?
**S**cope – How much information is it necessary to include?
**T**opic – Topic, as implied

Looking at the first letter in each element, you yield the word: **PAST.**

## Exercise C:

When stimulating your memory to remember vital information about a narration or a composition, you need to first take up the:

1. Composition
2. Remember it

3. Evaluate it
4. Analyze it
5. Think about it
6. Understand it
7. Review it
8. Express it.

Now take the first letters of each item on the list and form a word.

## ACROSTICS

Take a list and compose a sentence out of it. For example, using a list of countries, you might be able to compose a sentence employing the first letter in the name of each country. Take this list:

Hungary, Latvia, Austria, Spain, Slovenia, Turkey, Ireland, Montenegro, Macedonia, Czech republic.

Acrostic: **H**enry **L**umbers **A**long **S**o **S**lowly **T**hat **I**t **M**akes **M**e **C**razy.

Take this list of unrelated words: Trinket, Poses, Embryo, Hate, Empire, Brain, Irascible, and Yarrow. Compose a sentence from it:

Acrostic: **T**hinking **P**ositively **E**veryday **H**elps **E**mpower **B**elief **I**n **Y**ourself.

The order of the planets outward from the sun is: Mercury,

Venus, Earth, Mars, Jupiter, Saturn, Uranus, Neptune, and Pluto.

Acrostic: **M**y **V**ery **R**evered **E**ducator **M**umbled **J**ust **S**everal **U**seless **N**arrations **P**onderously.

For the four directions: North, East, South, and West:

Acrostic: **N**ever **E**at **S**quishy **W**orms.

Acrostics examples that you make up do not have to make perfect sense. If they are absurd, you may remember them better. For example, take a fact you want to remember:

Allergies to gluten result in celiac disease.

Acrostic: **A**bstract **T**echnical **G**hosts **R**ead **I**nnocently **C**reepy **D**arkness.

Stars are classified according to their spectral type. There are seven classifications: O, A, B, K, F, G, and M. Think of a silly sentence that starts with the first letter of the star classes.

## ASSOCIATIVE MEMORY

People can alter and add new networks of connections between memories and an unrelated stimulus. Altering these patterns is called neuroplasticity. To assume that your brain always remains the same throughout life because of your IQ is erroneous. This was a formerly held belief. Unfortunately too many people have jumped to the conclusion that their brain development occurs only throughout their childhood, and remain static after that. Neuroplasticity creates new neural paths not established in your earlier years. In that sense, your brain is not static.

A primitive example of associative memory is the association of "Green" with "Go" and "Red" with "Stop". However, people set up various types of associations throughout their lives. For example, suppose you meet a woman who uses an extremely strong perfume – a lavender scent – and it causes you to become somewhat nauseous. On the next occasion when you smell a lavender fragrance, you will recall that particular woman. Similarly, when you see that woman across a busy street, you will be reminded of the strong odor. You might even automatically become nauseous without being exposed to it. The association often goes both ways.

The senses play a vital role in associative memories. In the case cited above, it had to do with the sense of smell. It could just as well be sound. The famous behaviorist, BF Skinner (and others) taught animals to respond to a sound. For example, the ringing of a bell taught dogs that food was about to arrive. In response to merely the ring of the bell, the dogs would start salivating.

Memory in humans depends upon links and associations between objects regularly seen together. This indicates that the neurons have "learned" to create pathways that link one visualization with another.

Links can become complex. The odor of hot dogs cooking will remind you of a picnic. From there, you may remember the last picnic you attended. Then you will recall how one guy at that picnic was rowdy. Then you may remember other run-in's you have had with rowdy people. Then you may think of some other rowdy people you have known throughout your life...and so on. One memory gives rise to another.

## Exercises in Associations

**Exercise A:**

You need to remember a few important things to do for the day when you return from work. They are:

Pay Insurance Invoice
Wash and Dry Laundry
Buy garbage bags
Buy needle nose pliers from the hardware store
Call Leo

On the surface, there appears to be no relationship between the objectives; that is going to make it easier to forget one or more to-dos in the list. However, brains are "hard-wired" to think visually, so you can use a visual technique to remember these things. It is only going to be used from short-term or "working" memory.

Try this with the list above. Visualize a <u>washer</u> and a <u>dryer</u> in your laundry room. Picture yourself in there. On top of the washer, lies your <u>insurance invoice</u>. Into the washer, imagine yourself throwing <u>garbage bags</u>! From your dryer, imagine yourself taking out a pair of <u>needle nose pliers</u>! On top of the dryer, sits your friend, <u>Leo</u>.

## Exercise B:

If you need to fill your gas tank and pick up your shoes from the shoe repair guy, imagine pouring <u>gasoline</u> into your <u>shoes</u>!

## Exercise C:

Neuroplasticity in the brain, as discussed earlier, has to do with setting up new connections within the brain. For the following piece, the challenge is a tad more difficult, but the pattern of associations will be provided.

First, read this piece about writers in 20<sup>th</sup> century Japan, and you will set up a new structure of associations linking one fact with another and yet another.

---

Literary figures dealt with a myriad of issues. Some turned to traditional times for their creative ideas, while others were absorbed with international currents. Tanizaki Junichiro was famous for his book entitled the *Makioka Sisters*, a story of four sisters trying to survive in life after their domineering father died. Kawabata Yashunari had a stylistic preference for Heian writings. Using a psychological approach, he wrote some fiction pieces including the *Snow Country* and *Thousand Cranes*. Abe Kobo was famed for his narration called *Woman in the Dunes* for which he adopted a nihilistic point of view. Realistic war novels were the preferred themes for Ooka Shohei, as seen in his book *Fires in the Plains*. On the other hand, Noma Hirushi focused on the brutalities suffered by captured soldiers held in a military encampment. This was highlighted in her book titled *Zone of Emptiness.*

| Names | Books | Style/Theme |
|-------|-------|-------------|
| Junichiro | *Makioka Sisters* | Traditional |
| Yashunari | *Snow Country* *Thousand Cranes* | Psychological |
| Kobo | *Woman in the Dunes* | Nihilistic |
| Shohei | *Fires in the Plain* | Warlike |
| Hirushi | *Zone of Emptiness* | Military confinement |

What you need to focus on here is not recalling the entire narration, but three sets of data, categorized and classified. Your associations should be built up from associating a name with a book title and his or her style or theme when writing.

**Exercise D:**

Read this article about the Nobel Prize in chemistry, and then an associative diagram will be developed.

Three scientists won the Nobel Prize for their advances in a field that will trigger the development of many miniature machines and devices that will be helpful in computer development and the scientific field of physiology. A Frenchman by the name of Jean-Pierre Sauvage, a Dutch scientist, Bernard Feringa, and Fraser Stoddard, a Scottish scientist were honored for their work in creating devices that were extremely tiny - so tiny, in fact, that over 1,000 of them could line up inside the width of a human hair.

| Nobel Prize Chemistry | Sauvage Feringa Stoddard | Tiny devices for use in computer technology and for the human body |
|---|---|---|
| | | |

You may also create a silly sentence to help you recall the information:

Sauvage, Stoddard, and Feringa are three tiny scientists who won the Nobel Prize.

Their names, the word "tiny" and the words "Nobel Prize" would be sufficient information for you to commit the information to memory. Of course, you need to approach the task of reading with your undivided attention. Otherwise, you will not encode it properly, and fail to recall what the keyword "tiny" referred to.

**Exercise E:**

Read this story about two other Nobel Prize winners:

Composing contracts is a very challenging process. For their groundbreaking efforts in developing more effective and fair contracts, Oliver Hart from Harvard University and Bengt Holmstrom of the Massachusetts Institute of Technology, won the Nobel Prize in economics, which was awarded in October of 2016 in Sweden. Hart is from London originally and Holmstrom lives in Finland.

A silly sentence can be formulated associating the important information, i.e., the names of the men, their contribution, and their award. Silly sentence:

There was a <u>Fair and Effective Contract</u> between <u>Hart</u> and <u>Holmstrom</u> that won the <u>Nobel Prize</u>.

**Exercise F:**

Read this story and develop your own associative chart or silly sentence:

The Russian president, Vladimir Putin and Recep Tayyip Erdogan, the Turkish president, had their countries' energy leaders sign the "Turkish Stream" project, that is a pipeline that would carry gas from Russia into Turkey. It would then be distributed the nations that form the European Union. This event occurred at the World Energy Congress taking place in Istanbul.

---

**Exercise G:**

Read this piece and develop your own chart:

---

The Serbs are a Slavonic nation, and are similar ethnically to the Croats. The Croats, however, are Roman Catholics and use the Latin alphabet, while the Serbs belong to the Orthodox Church and use the Cyrillic alphabet, augmented by special signs for the special sounds of the Serb language. The first mention of the Serbs is to be found in the ninth century. Nothing is known of their earliest history except that they lived as an agricultural people in Galicia, near the source of the River Dniester. In the beginning the sixth century they migrated to the shores of the Black Sea. They dwelled there until the Emperor Heraclius invited them to settle in the devastated Northwestern provinces of the Byzantine Empire to defend the area from the barbarian invasions of the Avars.

# 5

---

# RELATIONSHIP OF ATTENTION
# AND MEMORY

There are many stimuli that impinge upon people on a daily basis. If all that stimuli is allowed entry into one's focus, the result is utter confusion and loss of control. Memory functions are hampered if a person does not limit the input. If you were to pose a challenging question to someone with a photographic memory, he/she would lapse into silence briefly. The person's facial expression would say: "I am thinking." If you say something further, that person will not even hear you! He or she has "shut off" all interference. That person has limited input into his or her mind.

Your experience may be different. For instance, you may be sitting on your desk, hearing traffic on the road, an airplane, and a bird tweeting. You may feel a breeze on your face from an open window, an itch on your arm, the nudge of your cat against your leg, and a drop of water on your head from a roof leak. You might see tree branches swinging in the wind, shadows falling on the lawn, clouds moving across the sky, and so on. Those are only the immediate sensations. You also have emotions that are stirring up within, some of which may be negative. Perhaps you are worried or anxious. Those emotional occurrences also qualify as interfering stimuli. Only the mind can select which stimulus or stimuli on which to focus. Only you can limit input into your mind.

Without the proper amount of input selection and attention, it is unlikely that the ability to remember will be improved.

## ATTENTION DEFINITION

Attention is a mental process by which some object comes to be apprehended more clearly and distinctly than all the other stimuli that are around. The effect of full attention is that a certain object is admitted into immediate consciousness, and the rest of the stimuli are relegated to the margins. If one concentrates on a song being played in the background, it may even seem louder, although in reality, there was no increase in volume. Attention affords one the opportunity to think clearly.

## PROCESS OF ATTENDING

William James, the psychologist and philosopher, is one of the primary theorists still referred to for his development of a theory relating to how a person must approach a task in order to increase his or her retentive powers. According to him: "It (attention) is the taking possession by the mind, in clear and vivid form, of one out of what seem several simultaneously possible objects or trains of thought. Focalization, concentration of consciousness is of its essence. It implies withdrawal from some things in order to deal effectively with others."

When encoding information and retrieving it later, James indicates that 5 functions must be activated:

1. **Take control** of your conscious mind.
2. Consider **ONE and only ONE** item at a time.
3. **Focus intently** on that item or piece of information.
4. **Withdraw** from other stimuli that invade your senses.
5. **Eliminate** distraction either physically or mentally.

There is no such thing as "multitasking"! No one can do more than one thing at a time. A person is not an octopus! It is true that one may have to do a series of related items at one sitting. However, the person can only focus on one of those items at a time. That is the nature of the human being.

## ATTENTION SPAN

A myriad of clinical studies has shown that an average person's attention span at any given period of time is only **eight seconds**! With some energy applied, a person can increase it to only around **twenty minutes**!

# TIMER

One technique is to employ the use of a timer. Set it to twenty-five minutes. Time to breathe. Take a few breaths. Relax. Then reset the timer to the next twenty-five minutes and keep plugging along.

If you break up information into blocks, you can accomplish much more.


# "WITHDRAWAL"

William James has said that one must "withdraw" from any stimuli that draws a person away from the matter at hand. In this day and age, that is even more difficult than it was in William James' time. Since the advent of technology and the computer, there is a conspiracy let loose upon the general public. While reading a computer screen, the person will be interrupted by a series of "beeps," pop-up ads, and talking videos to draw one's attention away from the task at hand. It is an effort, of course, to make money on the part of the intruder. Like needy children, they want you to do something you did not set out to do.


# ELIMINATION OF DISTRACTIONS

It is very challenging to shut out the distracting stimuli. Imagine that your mind is like a laser beam focusing upon the immediate item in front of you. Remind yourself that **you are the master** of the computer screen in front of you. Shut down, close off entrance to all the intruders. It is great to feel like you are the dictator of your private kingdom!

## THE "BULLY BRAIN"

Your own brain can betray your efforts to maintain attention. You don't even need the Internet to invade your desktop. Just beneath the cerebrum, the primary seat of your attention and focus are a number of structures that perform other functions. They compose what is called the limbic system. The limbic system monitors your instincts, mood, and emotions – the "Bully Brain". The hippocampus, as was mentioned earlier, is also located there. That handles your memory functions. You do not want the other aspects of the limbic system interrupting your memory functioning any more than you want the phone to ring while you are concentrating.

The "Bully Brain" will introduce urges into your conscious mind. The most difficult of these urges to handle are:

- Desire to eat
- Desire for leisure
- Desire for sleep
- Social impulses

In terms of your social impulses, you might be drawn to check out your Twitter feed, visit your favorite discussion group, read your email, make a phone call, and so on.

Teach yourself how to shut down those impulses until later on.

This will help you feel less guilty when the day is over.

**Create a New Schedule** for your next two blocks of time. You can employ the read/write learning style for this. Check off each item as you proceed down the list.

Also, plan out things you wish to accomplish later on.

## SHUT OUT THE DISTRACTIONS

Turn off your cell phone, and close down your email program. Shut the door to your office. Wear noise-cancelling headphones designed to stifle out environmental noises around you.

When you see those pop-up ads while visiting a web page, quickly snap on the "X" without reading it or looking at the pictures. Avoid noticing the sidebar on your right.

The ability to do this is called "cognitive control."

## THE EMOTIONS

It is a wonder how human nature has not changed over the years. All the way back in the 1st Century, a Latin writer by the name of Publius Syrus said: "Rule your feelings, lest your feelings rule you!" Wild and untamed emotions stampeding through your mind will result in turmoil, anxiety, stress, and tension. They will interfere with your focus and attention all the time.

Emotional IQ is the ability to be aware of one's own emotional state and learn to handle it, control it, and even reverse its negative effects. The term "Emotional Intelligence" was first coined by Salovey and Mayer in 1990.

Poor self-Esteem is the most debilitating of all your emotional needs.

Emotional Exercise A:

Make a list of all the negative things you do not like about yourself.

One of the most effective ways to overcome your negative emotions is by employing Newton's Third Law, which states that for every force, there is an equal, and opposite force.
NOW make a list of all the positive things you DO like about yourself. Work hard at this.

The brother of self-esteem is the need for the esteem of others.

To obtain the esteem of others, you need to become other-directed. You need to take the time to reach out and notice the other person. If you ask another "How do you do?" they will say "Fine." That is not enough to show your interest, so you add: "No, I mean how are you really doing? Now you have the other's attention, interest, and have increased their esteem of you.

Both self-esteem and securing the esteem of others will free you up so that you can more easily focus your attention upon the tasks that confront you. If you believe that you are not any good, or that no one else trusts or cares for you, it will place a severe emotional drag on your ability to focus your attention. Without attention to a task, the emotional barrage will interfere with your ability to remember and recall specific information. It will be like static on your radio. Who can listen to a tune when there is constant static? Chapter 7 in this book further addresses the relationship between emotions and memory.

## BREAKS

It seems obvious, though not always to some, that humans have an innate need for change. This can be just a simple trip to the coffee machine for a quick cup. Have you ever noticed that many open corporate office settings have a lot of empty desks? Where is everyone? They are walking around taking those breaks they so sorely need to break the monotony and spice up the routine. Do it yourself, although not to the extreme.

## INTERACTION, LISTENING, AND ATTENTION

In order to increase attention, it is necessary to listen first when material is being delivered verbally.

Take this recent interview with a radio announcer for example:

---

Announcer: "You have said that you're not going to allow British car manufacturing to be disadvantaged in the future. Can we agree that if they had to pay tariffs on their exports that would disadvantage Nissan and the other companies?"

Interviewee: "Well, first of all, just to endorse what you say, this is a big moment not just for Nissan but for the people of Sunderland. Talking to one of your colleagues this morning, they know people there. And it's my job to provide the assurances to Nissan and to other investors that Britain is going to continue to be a great place to invest in the future. I was able to do that, and this was the result that we saw announced this week."

Announcer: "Just coming back to my question then, would tariffs disadvantage Nissan?"

---

In this interaction, notice that the announcer was truly listening to the answers. He was focused and attentive. In his follow-up question, the announcer remembered his own question and evaluated the answer in light of that knowledge.

Consider this example:

---

Announcer: "How do you think this proposed gas task is going to affect the struggling middle class in this state?"

Interviewee: "Our roads and bridges have become progressively less safe to use by our middle class commuters due to their crumbling infrastructure. Many of those overpasses and bridges were actually built in the 1920s. In fact, we had to close the

Stickel Bridge over the Raritan Bay due to the weakening of the support pillars."

Announcer: "As a matter of fact, while on my way to the radio station, I myself was tied up in an enormous traffic jam because all the traffic had to rerouted to the Parkway Bridge."

---

Notice in the example above that the interviewee successfully dodged the question by producing only tangentially related information. He was able to sidetrack the announcer, who did NOT REMEMBER his own initial question, by losing focus and attention.

The other factor that looms large is the temptation to concentrate on one's next question (or answer), rather than actually listening to what was said first. People often make that mistake when they meet a new person at a social gathering. For example, they might ask a person his or her name. However, instead of listening to the answer, they are composing the next question to ask. Hence, the result is: "What was your name again?"

The well-known American novelist, James Patterson, once said: "I never miss a good chance to shut up." He has good listening skills.

# Tips to Increase Your Listening Skills

- Listen to the WHOLE message that a person is imparting.
- Watch his or her BODY LANGUAGE to determine the other's emotional intent while telling the story.
- Ask for a CLARIFICATION of what the other said. Never jump to conclusions. Those are usually based on your own experiences, not those of the other person.
- Interact with only ONE person at a time. That is similar to the suggestion earlier that multitasking is unrealistic.
- AVOID checking cell phones or other devices while listening to another.
- LEAVE YOUR SENSITIVITIES AT THE DOOR. Some people listen defensively possibly due to their low self-esteem. While they listen, they are on the lookout for something an individual says that may be construed (misconstrued) as a rub.
- AVOID TRYING TO COMPARE another's experience with something you yourself have experienced. This, too, is defensive.
- Use OPEN-ENDED questions.

With regard to open-ended questions, consider this example:

You are conversing with someone who is a baker by trade. You might begin by asking: "How do I thicken the peach mixture for baking a peach pie?" Forget your problem with the peach pie! Ask an open-ended question like: "What is your favorite food to bake?" Now you have the person engaged, and you gave him or her the warm feeling that you really appreciate the kind of work they do. In addition, you gave the other person the impression that you consider them an expert in matters related to baking. In addition, this reinforcement will help you recall the conversation. Another advantage of this is the fact that you can bring the subject up on the next occasion you happen to meet them. That is how friendships start. Relationships too!

You have effectively fulfilled your need for the esteem of others also. A nice bonus!

It is interesting to reflect on the fact that others may be just a tense as you are in a social situation where he or she may not know too many of the others. If you feel somewhat anxious, most likely other people feel that way too.

# 6

---

# TECHNIQUES FOR IMPROVING
# ATTENTION - MEDITATION

During wakefulness, your brain generates electronic waves called <u>beta waves</u>. You need those in order to function at work, and at home as you engage in various activities. The next brain wave pattern is a slower one called the <u>alpha wave</u> pattern. It is a waking pattern, but is more relaxed. Many people with photographic memories manifest this pattern much of the time. Meditation enhances alpha brain waves and a more relaxed mind.

## MINDFULNESS AND STRESS REDUCTION

Dr. Kabat-Zinn was the originator of the Mindfulness Based Stress Reduction program. Initially, it arose from the needs of patients afflicted with medical conditions causing pain and anxiety. Later, he discovered that the technique had a wider application.

In the years that followed that monumental finding, many scientists, sociologists, and psychologists have researched its effectiveness in the reduction of stress. In their study for the 2010 journal Emotion, Jha, Stanley, Kiyonaga, Wong and Gelfand found that the practice of Mindful Meditation "...may protect against functional impairments associated with high-stress contexts." According the their article for the *European Journal of Psychology*, their clinical results demonstrated that the positive effects of the regular practice of mindfulness meditation significantly reduces stress, including stress due to social anxiety. Self-acceptance, emotional empathy, personal growth, and self-improvement were enhanced. This proved to be true over a period of time.

## Mindfulness Meditation Exercise #1

1. Turn off your cell phone or other interruptive devices.
2. Take a glass and a small spoon that will make a tingling sound when you tap it on the glass.
3. Sit in a comfortable position on a soft chair or whatever you prefer.
4. Let your arms hanging loosely at your sides.
5. Tap on your glass gently.
6. Close your eyes, or simply cast them down.
7. Listen ever so carefully to your breathing. Breathe in and then breathe out gently. Listen; listen to the sounds of your breathing.
8. Feel the rise and fall of your abdomen as you breathe.
9. Concentrate on your body, and relax it little by little. Start with the toes, and then move up to the feet, the legs and so on.

10. Shift attention back to your breathing and listen.

11. Thoughts will intrude, little reminders of things on your "To Do" list. Accept the fact that those thoughts popped in, but focus your attention back to your breathing.

12. Feel the rise and fall of your abdomen. Every time a thought intrudes, accept it but do not dwell upon it. Return your attention to the sound of your breathing.

13. Listen ever so carefully to your breathing. Breathe in and then breathe out gently. Listen; listen to the sounds of your breathing.

14. Count while you inhale, and while you exhale. Continue listening and sensing the rising and falling of your abdomen.

15. Tap your glass with the spoon to announce the end of the meditation. (Do not forget to turn your cell phone back on!)

Continue this meditation for about fifteen minutes for your initial sessions. If you tend to fall asleep while doing this meditation, your body is telling you that you are getting insufficient sleep. Adults need to sleep for 7-8 hours a day.

## Mindfulness Meditation Exercise #2

1. If the weather permits, go outside on a starry night. Bring your glass and spoon with you, as you did for Meditation #1.

2. Sit in a relaxing position. Look up at the countless numbers of star hanging on a transparent curtain over deep space. Let your mind get lost in the wonder.

3. You will hear the sounds of night. Let them in and let them pass on. Other thoughts will interrupt you. Let them pass without thinking about those issues further. Focus, focus on the universe above you and "listen" to the silence of the sky. You are a part of the universe and it is within you.

4. Keep your head tilted backward toward the sky. Shut your eyes slowly.

5. Breathe slowly and listen to your breathing.

6. Feel your abdomen expand and contract. Listen; listen to your breathing.

7. Every time a sound is heard, accept it but draw your attention back to your breathing.

8. Breathe slowly and feel the night air enter and exit you. Sense your abdomen expand and contract.

9. Continue with this until you sink down to a soothing state of relaxation.

10. Open your eyes slowly and look at the star-speckled sky. Mentally sense yourself entering into the sky and place yourself among the stars.

11. You are a part of the universe and it encompasses you.

12. Maintain your breathing rhythm and hear the music of the sky.

13. Feast in that experience for a few more minutes.

14. Tap on your glass. The meditation is over.

## Mindfulness Meditation Exercise #3

1. Find a comfortable chair, but not too soft and billowy. Your back needs an adequate support.

2. Sit up, but do this in a position that is not painful or

strained.

3. Look at your right hand. Gradually tighten all the muscles, and make a fist. Hold your breath, and concentrate on that arm. Release it gently and exhale.

4. Focus on your right arm. Tighten all the muscles in that arm. Hold your breath and be sure you are looking at your right arm. Release the muscles and breath out.

5. Look at your left hand. Gradually tighten all the muscles, and make a fist. Hold your breath, and concentrate on that arm. Release it gently and exhale.

6. Focus on your left arm. Tighten all the muscles in that arm. Hold your breath and be sure you are looking at your right arm. Release the muscles and breath out.

7. Focus on your right foot. Lift up the toes and hold them up. Hold your breath and release the toes slowly, exhaling as you do so.

8. Focus on your right leg. Tighten your calves and your thighs. Hold your breath. Release those muscles gently and exhale.

9. Focus on your left foot. Lift up the toes and hold them up. Hold your breath and release your toes slowly, exhaling as you do so.

10. Focus on your right leg. Tighten your calves and your thighs. Hold your breath. Release those muscles gently and exhale.

11. Focus on your left leg. Tighten your calves and your thighs. Hold your breath. Release those muscles gently and exhale.

12. Tense up the back of your neck, raise your shoulders up, grit your teeth. Hold your breath. Then, as relaxing your neck, shoulders, and mouth, exhale slowly.

13. Sit in your chair. Drop your arms down at your side.

Relax and breathe normally.

## Mindfulness Meditation Exercise #4 – Also a Sleep Aid

This meditation can be used while you are seated. If performed in a lying position on your bed, it can function as a means to help you fall asleep. If you experience some uncomfortable sensations in certain parts of your body, like an ache or mild pain, accept that discomfort and move on to the next area in your body. If, by chance, you are in a LOT of pain, do not perform this meditation. You may experience warmth, cold, or tingling in the various parts of your body as you move through this experience. That is fine. It is helpful to play some gentle music during this meditation.

1. Close your eyes. Breathe normally and slowly throughout this meditation.
2. Focus on your toes and your feet. Relax them.
3. Now move up to your leg – first the right leg. Relax it totally.
4. Focus on your left leg. Relax that one too.
5. Sense both of your legs until they are totally relaxed. You will have very little feeling in them other than the fact that you are aware of their presence. If they are numb, that is even better.
6. Focus on your pelvic region and abdomen. Relax those areas as well. Be sure that your lower back is entirely relaxed. Avoid tensing it up or arching it in any way.
7. Relax your right arm and hand.
8. Relax your left arm and hand.
9. Check both arms to sense total relaxation in them.

10. Concentrate on your face. Sometimes people are not consciously aware of their forehead, but the muscles in it can be tensed as if you are worried. Be sure your forehead is relaxed as well as your cheeks and jaw. Let your jaw drop slightly if that is more comfortable for you.
11. If you are doing the seated form of this, open your eyes.
12. Move your arms. Then move your legs gently. Keep breathing normally and focus on your breaths.
13. Lift your legs up, one at a time.
14. Raise up your arms in front of you.
15. Gently rise to a stand and stamp your feet. If you are very good at this, they might have been asleep!

## YOGA

The origins of yoga date back to the 5th Century BC in India. In the Western world it is used for its physical and mental benefits. Mentally, it focuses upon union – the union of body and mind. Breath ("pranayama") is the major centering factor to get one's life into harmonious balance. Even though it is physical, it quiets an overactive mind that is often racing around from one thought to another. This reduces stress naturally. It is a far better substitute for tranquillizers if performed correctly. Mindfulness meditation discussed above is a Westernized offshoot of Yoga.

Some yoga practices advocate adherence to a set of beliefs, while others do not. Some people are aided by those spiritual elements, but it is unnecessary for those who do not wish to adopt a particular set of principles.

## POSTURE 1: SUN SALUTATION (Surya Namaskar)

1. Stand straight.
2. Put your hands in a prayer position. Inhale. Exhale.
3. Inhale and stretch your arms upward. Look up.
4. Exhale as you bend forward with your arms held slightly outward.
5. Breathe normally. Touch the floor and bend over as far as you can.
6. Bend upwards halfway placing your hands on your knees.
7. Put your hands flat on the floor and tilt your head down.
8. Bend your left leg out behind you.
9. Fold both your legs and bend down to the floor.
10. Place both your hands straight out in front of you.
11. Slowly return to your standing position.

## POSTURE 2: THE BRIDGE (Sethu Bandhasana-modified)

1. Lie flat on your back.
2. Bend your left leg and bend it at the knee. Keep it there.
3. Bend your right leg and bend them at the knee. Keep it there as well.
4. Put your arms straight out above your head.
5. Bend your arms with your palms backwards.
6. Lift your body in an arch-like position. Hold for a few seconds.
7. Slowly ease your body down and place both arms at your sides.
8. Rest for a while.

## POSTURE 3: SPINAL TWIST (Meru Wakrasana)

1. Sit on the floor. Stretch out your right leg.
2. Bend your left leg and put it over your right leg, foot flat on the floor.
3. Stretch your arms straight in front of you.
4. Raise your right arm up.
5. Twist the body to the left, placing your left hand behind so that it supports your weight. Turn your head and look behind you. Hold for a few minutes.
6. Raise your right arm up, then down.
7. Stretch out both of your legs in front of you.
8. Do the same thing with your other side.
9. Bend your right leg and put it over your left leg, foot flat on the floor.
10. Stretch your arms straight in front of you.
11. Raise your left arm up.
12. Twist the body to the right, placing your right hand behind you to support yourself. Turn your head and look behind you. Hold for a few minutes.

## POSTURE 4: HANDS TO FEET (Paschimothanasana-simplified)

1. Stand. Bring your arms out beside you, and then stretch your arms straight up.
2. Bend forwards slowly and touch the floor with your hands, palms down flat on the floor.
3. Put your head down.

4. Slowly come up halfway and hold this position for a few minutes.
5. Fold your body down and put your head down with your arms behind you, palms down on the floor.
6. Stand up *extremely slowly*.

## POSTURE 5: Corpse Pose (Shavasana)

1. Lie flat on your back.
2. Raise your arms slightly with your elbows outward and hands in a gentle fist.
3. Drop your arms to your sides.
4. Relax for a few minutes.

## POSTURE 6: LEG RAISE

1. Lie flat on your back on the floor or on a mat.
2. Focus your attention on the abdomen and lower back muscles. Be sure your lower back is flat on the floor and relaxed.
3. Inhale. Raise one leg up. Exhale. Lower that leg. Repeat 8 times.
4. Inhale. Lift the other leg up. Exhale. Lower that leg. Repeat 8 times.
5. Inhale. Lift both legs up together. Exhale. Let them down slowly.

# EASTERN-STYLE MEDITATION PRACTICES

The primary benefit of using the Eastern-Style meditation practices is the methodical elimination of the distractions caused by intruding miscellaneous thoughts that "pop" into the mind. It is an effective technique for mind control. As children, everybody was subject to a barrage of sensations, causing the mind to jump from one stimulus to another. The duties of everyday life in the 21st Century have aggravated this event, as there is so much information flowing into your mind. Technology has intensified this effect. When you visit a website, you are hit with many, many images and words. There is a benefit to this – you are "required" to filter out unwanted stimuli in order to gather the information you seek. Clinical studies have attested to this. However, if you are prone to snatching on to every exciting image or word, you are one of those who tend to "surf" the Internet in no particular order. Teenagers and children often fall victim to that. Every parent knows the detrimental effects on concentration when children and teens become disorganized and confused.

Like mindfulness meditation, the Eastern-Style meditations also bring attention to the breath as the unifying source. The creator of the Mindfulness technique, Dr. Kabat-Zinn, has studied Hatha Yoga in the East, which has influenced his style.

## PRACTICE 1: TRADITIONAL I

1. Sit with your legs crossed. If that is too difficult, sit in any posture that you find comfortable.
2. Rest your arms. Place your hands between your open

legs with the palms upward, fingers intertwined.

3. Close your eyes.
4. Listen to your breath. Inhale and exhale normally. Many thoughts will come to your mind, but let them float around your head like loosely floating bubbles.
5. Concentrate only on your breath.
6. Your breath will become thinner and shorter.
7. Slowly your breath will seem like it is settling in the area between your eyebrows. Your thoughts will diminish.
8. Sense a white or transparent blue ray coming from above. This is cosmic energy. Let it pour down on the top of your head; let it permeate your head and flow into your body. This is the "etheric body".

According to certain practices – for example, Theosophy – there are many forces surrounding the physical body. Those life forces around the individual correspond to themes, some of which are mentioned in this book. The physical, the emotional, and the mental forces are among those "bodies" that surround and permeate people. The theosophists talk of other forces beyond that, but that lies outside the scope of this book.

## PRACTICE 2: TRADITIONAL II

In this exercise, believe that you will move from untruth to truth. Inhalation and exhalation is of primary importance Breathing is at the heart of this meditation.

1. Inhale to the count of 4. Exhale to the count of 4.
2. Take 3 very, very short inhalations. While you are inhaling, extend your arms out in front of you.

3. Take 3 more very, very short inhalations. While you are inhaling, extend your arms straight out to your sides.
4. Take 3 more very, very short inhalations. While you are inhaling, extend your arms above your head.
5. Exhale, dropping your arms at your sides.
6. Rest for just a short time. Emergence from the Eastern style meditations should be gradual.

## PRACTICE 3: TRANSCENDENCE MEDITATION

1. Take a slow deep breath. Exhale slowly. You will start to feel lighter and lighter.
2. As you breath slowly, imagine yourself rising above the trees.
3. As you continue to breath slowly, feel yourself rising upward. You are surrounded by complete darkness. You are far away from your cares and worries.
4. Now sense yourself rising up until the age-old stars surround you. The stars saw you arrive, and they know when you shall leave.
5. Enjoy this space of nothingness among your companion stars.
6. Listen to your mind as it touches the transcendent. You will be given a new last name. It is among these: Faith, Hope, Leader, Charity, Humble, Kind, Strong, or Helper. Select one.
7. You will now be given a first name. It is: "I AM."
8. Say your new name – first name and last name. Pause.
9. Repeat your new name.
10. Focus on the nothingness among your companion stars. Hold that thought for as long as you can.

11. Come out of this meditation gradually. Work your way backwards through the steps.

# 7

---

# EMOTIONS AND MEMORY

## Emotions

Every mammal experiences emotions, including the human being. These are necessary for physical and mental survival. The physical aspects are clear – your body has the instinctual need to live and survive threats. The mental aspects are subtler. As sentient beings, mammals have the accompanying instinct for love, as first expressed by the parent(s), because the parent or parents are a source of food and protection. Some animals live a solitary life with the exception of raising a family. In their cases, once their young have reached adulthood, they go off on their own. The grizzly bear is an example of this. Other animals have the instinct to be accepted by a peer group. Apes, for example, seek acceptance by their extended family groups. They abhor being ostracized, and even develop compensations to alleviate the feelings of rejection that are associated with that.

The human being desires peer acceptance. Psychologists such as Abraham Maslow have called this the need for the esteem of others. One of the earliest experiences of childhood is a desire for peer acceptance. In the human being, the psychological need for love expressed by this acceptance can be termed "survival of the ego." It is mental survival, if you will, but survival nonetheless. Some emotions are positive, while others are negative. Even the negative emotions serve a function, because they direct you toward physical and mental survival. On the other hand, too many emotional intrusions stifle attention and memory functioning.

## A Word about Introversion

In reading the last section, some of you who are introverts may chide yourself. Introversion can be natural and normal for some people. Without the introverts, the world would be devoid of writers, musicians, artists, dancers, and many others. Introverts are not entirely isolated, regardless of society's general impressions about them. The human is a social being, but some people have less need for a lot of socialization. Emily Dickinson was one of the most famous poets of the 19th Century and she was infamous for being an introvert. That is expressed vividly in her well-known poem "I'm nobody. Who Are You?":

> "I'm nobody! Who are you?
> Are you – a Nobody too?
> Then there's a pair of us – don't tell!
> They'd banish us, you know.
>
> How dreary to be somebody!
> How public, like a Frog!
> To tell your name the livelong day

To an admiring bog!"

Dickinson "talked" to others through her writing. It is also interesting to note, that – after her death – her sister discovered hundreds of letters exchanged between Emily and a set of many friends!

## EMOTIONAL IMBALANCE

Using 3-step logic:

**Emotional imbalance causes stress.**

**Stress reduces memory functioning.**

**Emotional imbalance reduces memory functioning.**

Emotional imbalance causes stress, regardless of whether or not it is caused by too many positive or too many negative emotional experiences. It may be surprising to note that too many positive emotions have deleterious effects, as well as too many negative emotional events. In the case of an overabundance of positive emotions, a person might become manic, "hyper," and simply "too happy" to be considered normal. This is called the "Attention Deficit Hyperactive Disorder" (ADHD). It often occurs in children, but is also seen among some adults.

The detrimental effects of negative emotions are well known. Examples of those negative emotions are anxiety, depression, phobias and rage.

Emotional imbalance interferes with attention and memory. If your mind tends to jump from one thought to another unrelated thought, as in ADHD, you cannot focus your attention on one task. If you are depressed, anxious, or angry, you do not want to concentrate; however, completing a task involving memory and attention. Your motivation is ruined.

## 21st Century Sources of Stress

The breakneck pace of this 21st century world places huge demands upon its human population. Gone are the days when a person can saunter out of their dwelling, pick up a stick, knock a coconut off a tree, and enjoy a nourishing lunch. Survival today is based upon success as determined specifically by the various societies across the globe. The need for survival is not only a basic psychological need, but also an instinct. It determines how you live and move and have your being. Particular societies impose their own tailor-made expectations upon all adult human citizens of the countries in which they live. The normal reaction to meeting those expectations is stress. **Stress is normal, but excessive stress is crippling.**

Today there are more requirements placed upon people than ever before, and some people cannot fulfill all of them. A person must arrive at work at a certain time (or else!), get x, y, and z done before noon, then start over again in the afternoon. Failure to perform can adversely affect income, status, housing, medical care, relationships, and many other things, so there is a lot at stake. To make matters even worse, people are told that they must dress a certain way, act a certain way, have a beautiful body, and – in essence – to be perfect according to someone

74

else's standards.

## *The Adrenaline Rush!*

One of the most deleterious effects of this pressure plays itself out in your brain. In the hippocampus and the thalamus located in the center of the brain, and surrounding cranial tissue and nerves, memories are recorded. However, at the base of the hippocampus, part of that area, lie tiny bean-like structures called the amygdala. The amygdala regulates emotions through the use of neurotransmitters. In Chapter 3, the role of the neurotransmitters was elucidated. Stress causes an excitation of a certain neurotransmitter called epinephrine, also known as adrenaline. That particular neurotransmitter sends signals to the adrenal glands, then adrenaline is secreted, and adrenaline produces distinct physical reactions. Blood pressure rises, glucose (blood sugar) is pumped into the blood. In addition, muscles tense, a person's body is energized, and ready for self-defense. This may happen due to a physical threat such as the approach of an angry bear, but it also occurs when a person is challenged on a psychological plane.

When the boss storms out of his office and slams down a pile of product orders on your desk, insisting you have them processed in a hour, the **adrenaline rush** consumes your body and occupies your attention. While you are thus energized, you are also concerned about the failure to perform according to expectations. When a co-worker walks by and mutters a sarcastic comment, it happens again! When you get your e-mail and someone hollers at you from the Internet, it happens yet again! **STRESS** twice confounded!

Neurotransmitters are also packed into the amygdala, those structures in the brain relating to emotions. When the effects of negative stimulation elude conscious control, the emotions can overtake conscious functioning. This event was called the **"Amygdala Hijack"** – a term coined by the psychologist, Daniel Goleman, in 1996. In essence, this is the conquest of mental control by the emotions. If you are overwhelmed by emotions, memory functioning comes to a grinding halt.

## MEMORY? THE HECK WITH MEMORY!

After the neurotransmitters – norepinephrine and epinephrine – have caused the release of an overabundant supply of the hormone, adrenaline, you want to run away or you want to beat somebody up! Every reader of this book knows someone who has done that! Perhaps you are among those folks, at least on occasion.

Adrenaline has a "brother" hormone called **cortisol.** That is a natural steroid and its function is to shut down other bodily processes in response to the real or imagined threat. *Bye, Bye, efficient memory functioning!*
After a more mature reaction sets in – what was it again that you have to get done before noon? What else is on your plate for the morning? You missed your dental appointment. You forgot to call your daughter.

Once you have regained mental control, what are you going to do with all this excess adrenaline and cortisol? The added glucose adrenaline pumped in your system triggers you to eat.

Sometimes it urges you to eat and eat and eat some more! Obesity is often the unfortunate result. Stress must be reduced because you cannot function well with an unhealthy body being led by an unhealthy mind.

## *BURNOUT: A Potential Catastrophe Following the Adrenaline Rush*

Once the body's production of adrenaline has ceased, extreme fatigue sets in. That is accompanied by severe energy loss, clinical depression, despondency, hopelessness, and despair. A person in that state will lose all motivation, and work behavior will become simply a tedious, humdrum routine. A person thus afflicted may even give up a productive and rewarding career. In more extreme cases, a person may not even be able to work or raise a family. Some give up altogether and commit suicide.

In other cases, some adrenaline can be manufactured in the body briefly, and explosively surge into the bloodstream. When that happens people may be very prone to violence and rage. Usually, there does not seem to be any apparent cause for these episodes, and the violence is frequently directed randomly. No doubt, you have heard about those who have taken a rifle, and aimed it randomly at a crowd. When reading about those people, you may ask: "Why did he/she do it?" "What was his or her motive?" In truth, there was no motive. Tragically, it is just a **total loss of emotional and mental control.**

# SOLUTIONS

What can you do to bring about emotional balance?
What can you do to prevent or recover from burnout?

If you become more balanced in your emotional life, you can significantly improve your memory functioning. Improvement in your memory functions will motivate you to come even closer to achievement of a photographic memory, or at least come across like you have a photographic memory.

Yes, there are solutions for bringing about emotional stability. They are really not that difficult, but do require change. Change should NOT BE SUDDEN, because that is too traumatic. Everyone – *no exceptions* – can handle slight changes in their lifestyles, thinking patterns, and behaviors. Gradual change is the sure-fire way to make those solutions permanent.

## LIFESTYLE CHANGE

1. **MEDITATION** was suggested in the prior chapter. Initially, meditation sessions should be brief – very brief. You are not planning on becoming a monk! Monks and mystics manifest alpha brain waves much of the time, sometimes interspersed with slower brain waves called theta waves. Without joining a monastery, you can induce alpha and theta brain waves during waking cycles too. Those brain waves are peaceful and conducive to learning and memory. When the mind is manifesting the alpha wave pattern, it is on "input" – the mind is open to the input of information, images, new thoughts, creative

ideas, learning and memory.

2. **SLEEP** is essential to the reconditioning of the brain after its workout during the day. Everyone has experienced the effects of insomnia at one time or another. The effect is felt emotionally and mentally. Without sufficient quality sleep, a person cannot think properly, cannot remember things, and cannot function well physically.

3. **DIETS** need to be well balanced in order to maintain a healthy mind. There is such a thing as Brain Food! Certain foods help nourish the cells in the brain, making it ready for tasks that involve learning, attention, and memory. Some people experience excessive weight gain due to emotional stress. There are also foods that will help alleviate emotional imbalance and reduce the kind of stress that militates against memory functioning. These will all be discussed in the following chapter.

4. **ENVIRONMENT** is a major factor with relation to proper memory functioning. In Chapter 1, the various learning styles were delineated. A person with a <u>visual learning style</u> must limit the degree of visual input in the outside environment in order to use visualization primarily in the mind. People with the <u>aural style of learning</u> should not be bombarded with chaotic or unexpected noises in the outside environment. Soft music is conducive, but cannot be heard if it competes with other indoor or outdoor sounds.

Those with the <u>read/write style</u> will benefit from words, but not too many of them. It is challenging for those folks to limit the influx of words unrelated to the matters currently on their minds. Those folks find Internet pop-up ads most annoying. Those who have a <u>kinesthetic style of learning</u> need plenty of space. They may want to work out a preliminary industrial design using paper cutouts, boxes, or miscellaneous objects around them. They also may want to chew gum, suck on lozenges, or walk around the room without bumping into the furniture. Their environmental space should be quite open.

5. **SELF-DISCIPLINE** is the most vital need used in order to achieve happiness. Suppose you did develop a photographic memory, but you are a very unhappy person. That can and does happen. What is the point of being an eidetic wonder if you cannot use it to your own advantage? You are also rather useless in helping others too. You might be considered a show-off, too pedantic, boring, and difficult to socialize with. People will not want to associate with you, and that can cause emotional difficulties. Behavior and thought needs to be goal-directed. Without self-discipline, that happens only in certain areas of your life. There are myriads of examples such as research doctors or even marketers who are brilliant in their careers, only to see their marriages fall apart. They have let their obsessions control them and have sadly lost the discipline necessary to create a balanced life.

6. **EXERCISE** (Yikes!) helps your digestion and your bodily functioning, including your brain. It does not have

to be drastic. You are not planning on becoming an Olympic athlete. The objective is to maintain a healthy body guided by a healthy brain. The liver provides energy for optimal memory functioning by building up glucose. What happens if you do not use it all up? The leftover glucose is converted and stored in the body. Some of it may be stored as adipose tissue (body fat). Exercise helps burn off that excess, but it needs to be regular and consistent.

7. **HOBBIES** are not simply intended for retired people or children. Everyone needs them. If you really crave that photographic memory, you can adopt a hobby that will accentuate your memory functioning. It should not be related to your work; that is simply too much repetition. Sudoku is a number game published in many newspapers. It develops memory and attention. Learn a foreign language!* Memorization is required for that. Card games are also useful, but try to avoid Solitaire. You will master that in a very short period of time, and it does not grant you the opportunity for socialization. The other distinct benefit of adopting a hobby is the fact that it will help you relate to your family and friends. The old adage: "All work and no play makes Jack a dull boy" is true. Besides, your brain thrives on variety.

## *A Word about Foreign Languages

In looking for a hobby that stimulates the memory, it is suggested that you try to learn a language that is much different from your own. Those languages use different alphabets, and will help you develop new neural patterns in your brain. For those of you who live in the Western world, try to learn not only how to speak an Asiatic tongue, but also learn how to read and even write in that language. No, you may not be able to gain full mastery, but that is not your goal. A cursory knowledge of it is sufficient. It is a means to increase neuroplasticity in the brain; the forging of new neural networks. Those new neural networks can be applied to other mental activities as well. It is a different style of thinking.

By the same token, those who live in Asia would benefit from learning to read and write in some of those Western languages used in Europe, Africa, and the Americas. That creates new neural networks as well.

# 8

---

# LIFESTYLE

## Sleep

People who do not sleep well will not remember well, as most of you know from your own experience. In addition, insomnia causes emotional distress. That, above all, will interfere with memory.

There are five definite stages of sleep. In the chapter on Meditation – The Eastern-style meditations and the Mindfulness Meditations – it indicated that you could experience **Alpha brain wave** and even **Theta brain wave patterns.** Those are the same waves you experience in the First Stage of Sleep.

It helps to know what those stages are and **how they figure into memory retention.**

| Stages Happens | Brain Waves | What |
| --- | --- | --- |
| STAGE ONE | ALPHA, THETA | Restful sometimes. Called the "hypnogogic state". There may be interruptions by sudden vivid daydreams and noises. |
| STAGE TWO | THETA + Sudden "Sleep spindles" (non-rhythmic brain wave patterns) | Light sleep; heart rate slows. |
| STAGE THREE | DELTA waves | Realm of the Unconscious mind and body. You are entering deep sleep. |
| STAGE FOUR | DELTA waves more rhythmic | Physiological healing including restoration of brain cells and well as bodily healing and rest. |
| STAGE FIVE | ALPHA, BETA, THETA waves | * "REM" sleep. Dreaming occurs. |

# * "REM" Sleep: Role in Memory, and Dreaming

If you have ever recalled your dreams, have you noticed that activities you normally do or have done, and people you know appear in those scenarios? Of course, the stories make no sense.

*Note: If you want to partially analyze a recalled dream, your memory often substitutes one person for another. What your memory is doing is making associations between one person you know and another. Your memory sees likenesses between those individuals. That is one of the tasks of memory functioning. It was discussed in this book.*

Why do the stories make no sense? There are only speculative answers to that question. Try this:

## Possible Theoretical Explanation #1:

1. Go to a full Recycle Bin on your computer.
2. Browse through the entries.
3. Note that they do not make sense strung together. There is no logical connection between one entry and another.

Neurons in your neural networks, made up of pathways, may be haphazardly fired off.

## Possible Theoretical Explanation #2:

Your brain is repeating an issue you came across during your waking cycle. This can also reflect your emotional states such as frustration.

# YOU MUST HAVE REM SLEEP!

There have been countless clinical studies performed on the effects of a lack of this dreaming stage of sleep. When individuals are deprived of REM sleep for prolonged periods, they became less emotionally stable. In order for you to restore adequate memory functioning, you need to dream.

If you have trouble falling sleeping, try the Mindfulness Meditation Exercise #4. If you suddenly wake up in the wee hours of the morning, repeat that exercise. In extreme cases, try ½ tablet of an over-the-counter sleep aid. There are side effects to all brand-name sleeping aids, including dependency. Check with your health care provider if you have unusual symptoms including loss of memory.

## DIETARY SUGGESTIONS: "BRAIN FUEL"

Nerve cells (neurons) require Omega 3 fats ("good fats") to construct their cellular elements. Because your brain is a pack of neurons – of course – you should include plenty of these in your diet:

| | |
|---|---|
| Salmon | Walnuts |
| Canned fish | Oysters, Clams |
| Soybeans | Spinach |
| Safflower Oil | Olive Oil |
| Fish | Lentils |
| Peppermint (herb) | Papaya |

| Iceberg Lettuce | Anchovies |
|---|---|
| Flaxseed | Eggs |
| Almonds | Peanuts |
| Peas | Rice |
| Pinto/Navy Beans | Avocados |

Some butter substitutes have Omega-3 acid added. These are also recommended.

## DIETARY SUGGESTIONS: GLUCOSE DIGESTION

Memory usage will consume a lot of energy, especially for those of you who have taken up memory exercising. Your body will burn carbohydrates for fuel to perform those tasks. However, everyone is familiar with the problems that accompany weight gain. Those problems sometimes affect one's self image and serve as a total distraction from performing well mentally.

Adrenaline flow during extreme emotional agitation will also trigger you to eat. When adrenaline is shot into your bloodstream, it needs and uses blood glucose, a product from carbohydrates. Prolonged stress may produce an oversupply of blood glucose, however. What is not used by the body or stored in the muscles is converted to adipose tissue (body fat). That is one reason why stress needs to be dealt with in order to achieve an efficient memory.

# Those Duplicitous Carbohydrates

These molecules will help your body produce needed glucose. However, when it comes to the prevention of weight gain, certain carbohydrates should be avoided. That is because there are the kinds of carbohydrates that digest very, very quickly — causing your body to crave more. (And more and more)

There are other types of carbohydrates conducive to efficient memory functioning, and you will not feel the need to eat again quite so often. These will keep you satiated during study and memorization. Here is a partial list:

| |
|---|
| Whole grain pastas |
| Nuts |
| Beans |
| Brown rice |
| Sweet potatoes |
| Onions |
| Carrots |
| Green leafy vegetables |
| Oats |
| Whole grain vegetables |
| Fruit |
| Low fat milk products |

Sweets are carbohydrates, too, but should be eaten only in moderation.

# EASY EXERCISES FOR MEMORY ENHANCEMENT

These will raise your heartbeat and prepare you for memorization or study. Naturally, you do not have to do all of them during one session.

## Squats

1. Put your hands behind your head and interlock your fingers.
2. Squat down several times, rising up each time.

## Your Dance

1. Play a lively melody. Choose one that is rhythmic.
2. Imagine many colored lights swinging over you.
3. Also imagine an admiring and cheering audience watching you.
4. Dance! Move 4 steps forward, 4 steps backward, and 4 steps sideways.
5. Kick out your legs to the tune.

## Step Up

1. Locate a kitchen stool, a box strong enough to hold your weight, or you can use the bottom step of a stairway.
2. Step up with your right leg.
3. Bring up your left leg up to join the right leg.
4. Step down, one leg at a time.
5. Repeat this at least eight times.

## Punch n' Kick

1. Think of something that annoys you. Let it fester on your mind a bit. (This sounds silly, but it is effective!)
2. Stand with your feet somewhat separated. Put your hands on your waist.
3. Take four steps forward and punch out with your right arm.
4. Take four steps backward.
5. Take four steps forward and punch out with your left arm.
6. Take four steps backward.
7. Take four steps forward and kick out with your right leg.
8. Take four steps backward.
9. Take four steps forward and kick out with your left leg.
10. Take four steps backward. Repeat exercise if you wish.

## Burpees

1. Pretend you are in a battlefield! Take a chair and crouch behind it, like you are hiding from the enemy.
2. Suddenly leap up from behind the chair with your arms held up the air. (Like you are surrendering!)
3. Then leap down and crouch again. Repeat a few times.
4. Stretch out with your body slightly elevated off the floor as if you are going to do a push-up.
5. Suddenly get into a crouching position. Repeat a few times.

## Plank Jacks

1. Lie on your stomach.
2. Bend your arms. Be sure your arms are carrying the weight of your body.
3. Extend your two legs out behind you quickly. Repeat a few times.

## Seal Jacking

1. Stand in normal position.
2. Taking just one move, jump up and spread your legs outward. Bring your arms above your head simultaneously and clap your hands together.
3. Bark like a seal!
4. Return to your original position and repeat a few times.

This exercise is similar to the traditional jumping jack.

## Jump Rope

1. Take your daughter's jump rope and do a few bounces up and down.
2. This would be an exercise in and of itself and could replace the others.

# 9

---

## MEMORY RETRIEVAL

Much of your ability to remember depends upon **MOTIVATION.** If you want to come across like you have a photographic memory, you need to **REALLY, REALLY WANT TO COME ACROSS LIKE YOU HAVE A PHOTOGRAPHIC MEMORY!** See the difference?

During the course of a day and a week, everyone engages in little tasks that require a certain number of parts.

### VISUAL CUES

This is just a very simplistic example. The reason for this simplicity is the fact that – by doing this – you will get in the habit of doing it for more advanced tasks. Use this technique for simple tasks, and you will learn how to use it for more advanced challenges, whether they are physical or intellectual.

You are cutting up a cardboard box with and Xacto knife. You have placed the box on the floor and set the Xacto knife alongside. Then you are flattening out the box. Next you reach for the Xacto knife. Whoooops! It is not there! Where did you put it down? (Search starts…) Does that sound familiar?

## Cue Instillation

Run through the same scenario as above. However, when you put the X-Acto knife on the floor, pause a split second and say aloud (or to yourself): "I am keeping the X-Acto knife here." Look at the spot; commit that spot visually to your memory. Initiate your task, but every time you put down the X-Acto knife, go to the trouble of returning it to the same spot. Easy-peasy!

**Cues** are also hints. If you have to read and study a number of documents, pause after reading each one, and ask yourself "What is the name of the article? What does is have to do with?" For example, let's say that you read a document called "Windows to the Stars" that discussed the various types of telescopes. At the end of studying it, pause. Ask yourself: "What is the topic of 'Windows to the stars'?" Keyword: "Telescopes". That cue is like the first few notes of a melody. Once you hear the first few notes, you can sing the rest.

**Recollections** are larger pieces of information that you remember given the initial cue. In the example above, your cues were "Windows on the Stars," and "Telescopes". Telescopes you studied were: reflector telescopes, Dobsonian telescopes, binoculars, and compound telescopes. That is sufficient for you to compose a short article or essay about the contents of your study.

**Timing:** Earlier, this book discussed the Ebbinghaus Cycle of Forgetting. Because the process of memory decay sets in very soon, the material needs to be brought to mind again within 1-4 hours since it was first encoded. This reinforces the information, and it will be retained for a longer period of time. This is sometimes called "overlearning" or "relearning."

## ROOM STRATEGY

Enlist the aid of a visual help. In this case, it is a room. With regard to the article the person read about telescopes, he or she could think of a room. Into that room, the person can imagine the various types of telescopes, and have them mentally labeled. This is just a simple example, but you can use it for more complex material. You can always expand the house to include many rooms, in which you have different items. The items can even be words that act as cues for more complex material.

# CONTEXT AND RECALL

The senses are all encompassing. Although you may not pay much attention as to where you were when you first learned the information, the environment in which you learned the facts is very influential in memory retrieval and recall. The surroundings make a tremendous difference. If you are studying in silence, then you should take a test in school in silence, rather than putting your headphones on. Sometimes alteration of a place can induce memory failure. For example:

> *Herb is walking through a big box store in the hardware department. A woman approaches. "Hi, Herb! How are you? I have not seen you in a while. When are you coming in again?" Herb looks at the woman in total confusion.*
> *"You don't know who I am do you?" she asked.*
> *"No, I am sorry. Who are you?" he responded.*
> *"You do not recognize me outside the dental office, do you? I am Loretta, your dental hygienist!"*

What Herb did was to fail to remind himself of experiences in the dental office, including the faces of the personnel there. He may easily remember the dentist by facial appearance, but overlooked the importance of encoding everyday events in more detail. He could have left the dental office on his last visit and taken a few moments on his way back to his car to rehearse the faces of the people in the dentist's office at the time, in addition to his dental procedure, rather than banish the whole episode from his mind's eye.

Training your mind to become like that of a person with a photographic mind includes the <u>careful study of everything that</u>

occurs during the day in great detail – including the inconsequential and trivial. Here is an example of incomplete encoding of information as discussed in Chapter 1: What if you went to a new neighbor's door with your mother and saw a little decorative wooden bear by the door holding a Welcome sign. And your 82-year old mother says: "Oh, Vivian down the street has one like that!" In the meantime, you are clueless, and embarrassed as well!

Returning yourself at least by way of **visual** imaging will help you recall information received. For those who learn best under **auditory** stimulation, one can play a song while working on a particular informational piece. Then, playing that same song while reproducing that material will help with recall. This is also based upon associative memory.

## STIMULANTS AND MEMORY

Some students unfortunately have taken drug-based stimulants to help them study. While this method seems to work, of course, dependency upon the stimulant can occur. In addition, habitual use results in the opposite effect. Drugs like amphetamines destroy brain cells, and ability to remember over the long term is adversely affected. Coffee does aid in memory, although individuals must be careful about the amount of it taken into the body. Too much can produce hyperactivity and raise the heartbeat to excess. Tea also has caffeine, but has been shown not to always have the same side effects. It tends to be sipped as opposed to being gulped.

As an alternative, it would be far better to try out memory-boosting supplements addressed later in this chapter. They are safe and harmless, and are not addictive.

## The "Tip of the Tongue" -"TOT"- Phenomenon

This is a familiar phenomenon that happens to many people, particular those who are older, according to clinical studies. Of course, the other factor irrespective of age is the passage of time. If an even occurred two months ago, it will be more likely to be retrieved than an event that happened a year ago. No one can go over the events of an entire year frequently. Hours in the day prevent that from happening. It is amusing to note some dialogue often heard in a TV show or movie when a police detective asks a suspect: "Where were you Monday two weeks ago?" Oddly enough, scriptwriters frequently have ready answers for their actors for these questions!

The best solution for the "Tip of the Tongue" occasions is to immediately move your mind on to another issue. Very often, the answer "pops" into your mind just a few minutes later. Due to the neuroplasticity of the brain, a nerve pathway has been stimulated and keeps itself subtly activated until the final outcome registers in the prefrontal cortex, the conscious center of your brain. Emotions should never be injected in the situation, however. One should never permit himself or herself to "feel bad" about the failure to recall the answer immediately. Emotions will always interfere with memory functioning, as explained in Chapter 7.

# Failure to Replace the Old with the New

In his research, Hermann Ebbinghaus (The "Forgetting Curve") indicated that when one studies lists in particular or like sets of data, any alteration of the list inhibits memory retrieval. If one studies twelve items, for example, recalls them, and later takes that same list, replacing two or three items with something different, memory is adversely affected. A good example of this is the channel listings on the TV. Once the channel numbers have changed, a person tends to remember the old numbers rather than the new numbers. Not only is this a deficit in relearning, but also a failure in the initial coding process used. Extra effort needs to put into the relearning task. Otherwise, Americans would be driving on the wrong side of the road in a rented car for a vacation in England. This often happens.

Change is a source of aggravation that increases in proportion to age as well. Older people resent having to learn the basics of computer use. However, it is also manifest in children as they attend school and have to function differently as they move on from one grade to another. Some children have been known to shout out: "Why do I have to go through all these changes?" when they are required to move about the building for their various classes instead of staying in just one classroom.

# Review

As indicated earlier, a review of the facts or information within a few hours up to a day after learning (encoding) takes place will improve your chances of placing those facts into a long-term or at least longer-term memory situation.

Recall Exercise:

In Chapter Two of this book, a few passages were presented in an exercise. The theme was the cultural/ethnic heritage of the Arab world. (Cue!) In that interest, see if you can answer the following question:

Who are the Copts?

Do not flog yourself if it so happens you do not remember. Go back, and review it. In two days' time you still remember the answer, and perhaps even longer!

## FALSE MEMORIES

Even innocent light emotions influence recall. A person can relate an incident to another, and note that the incident evoked a positive reaction on the part of the listener. This is a reinforcement of the memory, in which case, the person tends to remember the incident so he or she can retell the event to another, hoping to elicit yet another positive response. This is very obvious in joke telling, but can happen with any event.

In time, that person may embroider the incident a bit, perhaps adding a few details that make it more interesting and amusing. After a while the person may come to believe it as it was most recently related.

Influence is also a factor. If someone wants you to relate an event a particular way, you may repeat it in order to please that person. In time, you yourself come to believe it, rather than the fact that someone else told you to do it.

## THE OVERCONFIDENCE FACTOR

This is also called the "Foresight bias," and it was delineated in the studies of Koriat and Bjork. These two cognitive psychologists indicated that that people tend to be overconfident and fail to make an extra effort to learn or encode information when first presented with it. How often have you heard this dialogue?

"You should write this down in case you forget it."
"Oh, I will remember it…no problem."

Then, when the time comes for that person to retrieve that piece of information, what happens? He or she forgets it! First of all, the person assumed that the fact(s) would be simple to remember. Assume nothing! The memory is like moving an object from its old established place in your house and placing it elsewhere. Then, when you try to retrieve it, you cannot recall where you put it. You might remember the original place, but did not put enough effort into learning the new place. It represents the failure to replace the old with the new.

# MEMORY BOOSTING SUPPLEMENTS

In some studies, the supplement, *Ginkgo biloba* has been shown to help. Its physical effect is to increase blood flow. Many older people use this to help them allay or prevent the onset of dementia. In that area, it is less effective according to clinical results, but has a better efficacy for others who are younger.

Ginseng, which can be used as a tea, and turmeric, an Asian spice is helpful. Both of these can be grown in your herb garden. Both are available in the health food and grocery stores. They have a long history of medicinal usage going back through the centuries to India and China.

Vitamin E is also effective, but should not be taken too frequently. Some vitamins are not immediately flushed out of the system if not used by your body. One can actually overdose on those. Vitamin B (thiamine) is often recommended to reduce anxiety. However, a person can overdose on it, even with a once-per-day schedule.

Others that are recommended are: Alpha GPC supplements, Bacopa, citicoline, curcumin, and magnesium supplements. It is best to use these with caution and avoid daily intake.

# 10

---

## APPLIED MEMORY

### Remembering Names

*"There is no sweeter sound to any person's ear than the sound of their own name." – Dale Carnegie*

Dale Carnegie was a writer and speaker whose premier message was about how to appeal to others. He was a public speaker who taught the craft to millions over the years. In business and communications, memory is of the utmost importance. One needs to reach out to others, because self-fulfillment and basic happiness is not achieved in a vacuum. The first step in reaching out is attaining a mastery of other peoples' names. There are many memory tricks one can enlist to achieve this.

One of the most powerful tools is a visual one. When you are introduced, imagine a person's name emblazoned on their foreheads. You may add an auditory element by accentuating the last syllable and saying the name silently to yourself with the accent:

| LEON | ANNA | DOUG |

## RHYMING TECHNIQUE

Once you hear a person's name, match it to a rhyme. For example:

| Abel Table | Al the Pal | Adam Macadam | Drew Knew |
|---|---|---|---|
| Artie's Party | Samir Premier | Ben (is) Ten | Kyle with Style |
| Bill's Will | Bruce the Deuce | Clare Dares | Ricky the Tricky |

## ASSOCIATIVE TECHNIQUES

Sometimes you might remember better if you associate a physical or personal characteristic. In your first conversation with a person you have not met before, it is very complementary to repeat the person's name during your first conversation. After a longer conversation, the association can easily be dropped.

For example, you meet a woman at a party by the name of Melanie. She is hanging on to her boyfriend, John, as she speaks with you. You can now associate Melanie with romance, so Melanie becomes "Melanie Romance" in your mind. Her beau is John, who is wearing bright white sneakers. He is "John the Sneaker."

Try these associations (in your own mind, of course):

| Charles the Bald | Sammy the Hat |
|---|---|
| Tamika the Sleeve | Ronnie the Small |
| Malcolm the Neutral | Marion the Sad |
| Leroy the Cell Phone | Geoffrey the Brain |

The associations can be the opposite of a person's most prominent characteristic. For example, in the above chart, Ronnie is NOT small; he is of a massive size. Geoffrey appears to be the intelligent type just from his appearance. Tamika has a tendency to adjust her sleeve when she first meets anyone. Sammy arrived at the affair wearing a hat. Marion's facial expression appears to be melancholy; and Malcolm's face seems to be without expression. Charles, of course, is bald (but you do not tell him so!)

## The Written Name

Naturally, you cannot write down or record everyone's name at a gathering. That is being too obvious. However, you can subconsciously improve your appreciation of the importance of noting someone's name with strangers on your telephone.

Everyone has had calls from their banks or agents working for a company with which you do business. They do introduce themselves by their first names. Write the name down. As you engage in the business issue with them, *say* their name. If you are trying to persuade them to do something your way, this is *extremely effective*.

## Review

At the beginning of an affair, engage someone or a few people in a conversation, and repeat their names. After you are seated and situated, glance over their faces, and review their names in your mind again. If you do not recall some names, you can ask someone nearby (whose name you do remember) what that person's name is.

# SEATING APPROACH

Have you even noticed how people at a party tend to "claim" one seat for themselves? Even after going to another room briefly, they return to the same seat, which has politely been left vacant for them. You can make a "seating chart" in your own mind. Teachers use those at the beginning of every school year to help them recall the names of the children in their class.

See the image below:

# ATTENTION AND SELF-DISCIPLINE

The role of **attention** was addressed earlier in this book, but is a major helpmate in remembering peoples' names. Instead of thinking what you are going to say next to someone, think instead of the technique you have chosen to recall a person's name. This takes practice and self-discipline but carries its own reward at the end.

Most people are very concerned about how they come across to others, but the more important factor in memory is to focus upon something you did not already know. That is not found inside you; it is found in the other. Ask open-ended questions about others, encouraging them to talk. You can also review their names at the same time. This system is a win-win formula. The others will feel good that you are interested in them, giving you a sense of the esteem of others. As the other people smile, you will feel good about yourself as well. That is self-esteem. The best reward of all is that you may have the opportunity to learn something you never knew before. For example, should you happen upon a beekeeper, he would be ever so happy to share some of his knowledge with you. That gives you information you can store away in your memory to use at the next social gathering. People will marvel at your knowledge!

**Self-discipline** in the realm of daily living is characterized by a schedule. Every day, perhaps even more often, it is recommended that you develop a schedule. Unrelated items may be listed, and that is a good test of memory functioning as well. Time management experts always indicate that everyone should set a time allotment for each task and tuck the obligations he expected of himself into those time segments. Warren Buffet, the well-known billionaire, advocated following a routine. His memory was excellent, as this routine system freed up his working memory to direct his attention to various tasks at hand. A relaxed mind is more conducive to fostering a well-oiled memory.

The need to reject emotional intrusions is also critical.

Procrastination is generally considered self-defeating, but can be harnessed to control urges like grabbing a snack, sleeping in, making an unnecessary phone call, or succumbing to the alluring call of Twitter and other social media tools. Any interruption disturbs memory functioning when you are in full swing. Those are the nasty habits of your "bully brain" attempting you to divert your attention away from the matter at hand.

## DOODLE AND FRECKLE TECHNIQUE

While doodling may seem like a distraction, it can be an aid. In the graduate school of an Ivy League university, a very clever woman by the name of Donna used to doodle whenever she studied for very complex examinations. For one particular exam, Donna recorded every topic and major subtopic in ten chapters in the form of a doodle. As she reviewed the material, she used to study the doodles and the significance of each one. One day, as she was about to take an exam, she brought her sketchpad with her – loaded with doodles. The exam was of the multiple-choice variety, but she was confident. As she proceeded to mark her answers, she referred to sections of her doodle drawing. Because her eyes were moving back and forth from the test paper to the doodle sheet, the professor approached her desk to look on. He, of course, suspected she was cheating. Of course, all he saw was a page of doodles! Donna graduated the school *Magna Cum Laude!*

Likewise, you can employ aids like this. Seamus from Ireland used to use the "freckle" trick. Because of his ethnicity, his arms were full of many freckles. As he tried to remember items, he checked with the freckles on his arm for reference.

The "Doodle and Freckle Technique" utilizes your associative memory skills. Most people learn from association; it is basic to the human species.

It only remains to say now that the father of memory is practice. According to Vladimir Horowitz, the famous violinist: "The difference between ordinary and extraordinary is practice."

# CONCLUSION

The memory centers in your brain engage in the triple functions of Encoding, Storage, and Retrieval. As you are mentally processing data, you walk amid two worlds – that of the body and that of the mind...that which is tangible and that which is intangible. It is a mysterious phenomenon only known to humans. Pasts and presents race before your mind's eye, and time is the only variable.

Every learning experience in your life has value. Although it may not mean much at the time, it is an incredible journey to make an indelible record of your life's experiences. This is something you can share with others. Be proud always of who you were and of your internal encyclopedia and autobiography. No one has experienced the memories that you have, and so you are unique.

Do not permit time to extinguish those memories. Exercise that precious part of your mind; nurture it as you have learned in these pages, and your memory will serve you well. There are thousands, perhaps millions of people seasoned by years and years of experiences who can remember names, dates, places, skills, and talents they developed over the years. Some people have even remembered events they have experienced before they were one-year old! If you respect all of who you are, you too have such a photographic memory that people can admire and covet.

# About the Author

Stefan Cain has spent the majority of his working career in numerous academic research positions, working on a wealth of psychological, societal and cultural topics. His research work and adept studies have been used to form the backbone of many popular titles available today, providing him with the experience and hunger to delve deeper into some avenues of thought.

Alongside his serious academic work, Stefan has been published in a number of prominent publications; filing news reports, features and insightful opinion pieces on myriad topics throughout his career. It was here, in this capacity as a journalist, that he first began to start writing about human behavior.

Made in the USA
Lexington, KY
08 February 2018